THE
BLUE BLOODS
COOKBOOK

THE
BLUE BLOODS
COOKBOOK

120 Recipes That Will
Bring Your Family to the Table

BRIDGET MOYNAHAN *and*
WENDY HOWARD GOLDBERG

with CHRIS PETERSON

ST. MARTIN'S PRESS
NEW YORK

THE BLUE BLOODS COOKBOOK. Copyright © 2015 by Bridget Moynahan and Wendy Howard Goldberg. All rights reserved. Printed in the United States of America. For information, address St. Martin's Press, 175 Fifth Avenue, New York, N.Y. 10010.

www.stmartins.com

Designed by Susan Walsh

The Library of Congress Cataloging-in-Publication Data is available upon request.

ISBN 978-1-250-07285-6 (hardcover)
ISBN 978-1-4668-8480-9 (e-book)

Our books may be purchased in bulk for promotional, educational, or business use. Please contact your local book-seller or the Macmillan Corporate and Premium Sales Department at (800) 221-7945, extension 5442, or by e-mail at MacmillanSpecialMarkets@macmillan.com.

First Edition: November 2015

10 9 8 7 6 5 4 3 2 1

WENDY **GOLDBERG**

This book would not exist if it weren't for Leonard Goldberg, the creative force who developed Blue Bloods…and so smartly put in the family dinner. Thank you, dearest husband, father, and best friend.

BRIDGET **MOYNAHAN**

I'd like to thank my mother, who taught me how to cook and bake. Thank you to my father and brothers, who are patient with my numerous calls and questions every time I cook a big dinner. To Uncle Charlie, for cooking with me anywhere, anytime. Lastly, to Brotha D, who made that call almost seven years ago, and Leonard Goldberg, for taking the chance on me.

CONTENTS

ACKNOWLEDGMENTS

To Chris…our superhero, whose expertise, wisdom, and good sense have contributed immeasurably to this project. Thank you…we couldn't have done it without you!

This book has been a collaborative effort and we owe many people our heartfelt thanks. Leslie Moonves is an extraordinary leader whose talents have no limits. Thank you so much, Les.

We also owe a big debt of gratitude to *Blue Bloods'* resident guardian angel, Jane Raab, who is the heartbeat behind the scenes of the show.

Steve Cohen championed the book from the very start, understood our vision, and was tireless in keeping everything on track.

More thanks to Kevin Wade and the *Blue Bloods* family, who contributed recipes, time, and thoughtfulness along the way. Many thanks to Jillie and Tom Selleck, Heather and Len Cariou, Donnie Wahlberg, Will Estes, Amy Carlson, Sami Gayle and Robin Klitzman, and Andrew and Tony Terraciano.

We sincerely appreciate the amazing work and consistent high quality that editor Elizabeth Beier and editorial assistant Anya Lichtenstein brought to the project. You guys rock, not least for bringing in Ben Fink's spectacular photographic talent. Ben, Joe Tully, and Lori Powell—thank you for creating images that brought the recipes to life in the most vibrant (and hunger-inducing) style.

We'd like to acknowledge, as well, the efforts of Toni Howard, Lynda Resnick, Jonathan Anschell, Marcy Morris, Kimberly Jaime, Andi Nichols, Richard Boeth, Lauren Santiago, Bernard Jazzar, Belen Mirisch, and Edna Garcia.

Lastly, we'd be remiss to leave out Jaime Toporovich, who is the glue that holds so much together, including the moving pieces involved in making this book. Thank you, Jaime!

All meals created with much love for Jack, Grace, Vincent, Sophie, Cecelia, and Josephine.

THE
BLUE BLOODS
COOKBOOK

INTRODUCTION

Every episode of the TV show *Blue Bloods* includes a family dinner scene. The main characters gather around a big oak table in the soft light of a spacious old-fashioned dining room to eat a leisurely dinner that everyone takes turns making and serving. They all sit there together talking, laughing, and hashing out the latest dramas in their lives. As a TV family of cops, the dramas are large and small: from a current kidnapping case in the news to everyday money troubles. No matter what the issue, though, the family dinner offers a perfect stage to work everything out.

It's a simple and wonderful tradition. As two family-oriented women—one a star of the show, and the other the wife of the executive producer—that tradition means a lot to us. We've both seen the magic of the family dinner firsthand. It's how we were raised, and something we have tried to institute in our own homes, with our own families.

The family dinner was intentionally written into the show as a centerpiece and a dramatic anchor. It's a great narrative device and a lot of fun to film. But we think viewers connect with that particular scene for reasons other than how well it helps resolve the plot of each episode. When you read as many viewers' letters and online comments as we have, you begin to understand that people cherish that scene—and the ritual it represents—in a very deep and profound way. It goes beyond the love of the show, beyond any given episode.

Let's face it—the world moves very fast these days. Our lives really are busier than ever before. There's a lot of noise in the world. Everyone is in a hurry. So is it any wonder that the very simple idea of just stopping for a moment in time, sitting down to eat a satisfying meal, and perhaps having a casual discussion about nothing and everything strikes such a deep chord with all kinds of people?

We're convinced that everyone would be happier if they nurtured their own family dinner tradition. It starts with the people. As two mothers, we can tell you the real challenge is getting those people to the table at the same time. "Too busy," they'll say.

ON THE SET . . . **WITH BRIDGET**

By the end of season five on *Blue Bloods*, we had filmed 111 dinner scenes. That's a lot of food faking! When you're filming a scene that involves eating, the key is to make it look natural take after take, and hopefully not talk or chew with a mouth full of food. For the first few seasons, I would smash my food around my plate. Amy Carlson—who plays Linda Reagan—is always cutting her food. Tom Selleck had the best move from the start: buttering rolls. I still wish I made that my move first. It's easy, natural, and you don't have to eat! It's amazing how much on-camera time you can take buttering your bread. I tried to convince Tom, my TV dad, to let me take his dinner action over. No such luck. He knows when he has a good thing.

"I'll just grab a bite while I'm out." You can talk all you want about reconnecting as a family and spending quality time together, but trust us, just wanting it to be so isn't going to work. No, there's only one thing that is guaranteed to get the people you love to the table you set—food!

Delicious, filling, soul-satisfying, loosen-your-belt food is the main attraction of any family dinner. People can wear jeans. The house can be a mess. The table can be set with plain old flatware. But the food has to be special.

That's why we wrote this book. We knew from experience that the smell of a properly cooked pot roast straight out of the oven is a dinner bell that no mortal can resist. We're keenly aware that a blueberry-topped cheesecake made with equal parts love and cream cheese will make leaving the table "to go meet my friends" next to impossible. So we dug deep into our own family recipes, reached out to friends for their favorites, and did a whole lot of research to collect those dishes that are most ideally suited for a hallowed place on the family dinner table.

These are classics that have graced family dinners throughout time. We've taken pains to include something for every occasion a family celebrates, from average weeknights to cocktail parties. Each of these recipes is meant to please a person on many different levels, touching the heart every bit as much as the stomach. They are comforting, fun, delicious, and, for the most part, easy to make. To make them even easier, we've included some tips and kitchen strategies throughout the book, which you can use to save time spent in the kitchen (more to spend with the people at the table!).

We've even included a short collection of memorable menus that will help you plan any special occasion (*Blue Bloods* Family Dinner Menus page 255). We've tried to do everything we could to make it as easy as possible for you to gather your tribe around the dinner table—short of cooking the food ourselves!

Keeping in mind that the family dinner that started this whole ball rolling occurs in every episode of the *Blue Bloods* TV show, we've sprinkled stories throughout the book, describing what happens behind the scenes and on the set. Whether you're already a fan or not, we think that you'll probably smile at the legendary tales about Tom Selleck's dislike of anything that might resemble a vegetable or a salad, and Donnie Wahlberg's larger-than-life personality.

So call and let everyone know when dinner will be served, set the table, and start cooking! It's time to recapture the ritual of eating a fulfilling meal with the ones we care most about. This book is from our tables to yours, with humble wishes that you eat, share, and love.

Bridget Moynahan   Wendy H. Goldberg

BEHIND THE SCENES . . . **WITH WENDY**

My husband, *Blue Bloods'* executive producer Leonard Goldberg, developed the family dinner scene as a hallmark, a recurring scene that would tie every episode together. But he likes to say it was also part of a big error he made on the series. As he describes it, "The very first day we were going to shoot, I planned to do the first family dinner scene. That was a mistake. Normally, you wouldn't start off a show filming a scene like that because it calls for the actors to have very easy and natural relationships with one another. The audience has to believe these people have been meeting like this their whole lives. But, of course, in reality the actors had just met. So with one day of rehearsals, we shot the family dinner scene. Fortunately, all the actors were totally comfortable with one another. That's when I knew we had something special, because they all just clicked."

SOUPS

FRENCH ONION SOUP

*If decadence were a soup, it would be French onion. This cold-weather favorite includes an ensemble cast of flavors ruled by the sublime, caramel sweetness of sautéed onions. Each ingredient plays a part, and if you want the best bowl of soup possible, don't skimp on any of them. The melted Gruyère cheese is meant to top the bowl, the baguette, and the soup beneath, but sends the entire production over the top flavor-wise. It's just the type of simple, unpretentious, but wonderful creation you'd find on an Irish police commissioner's dinner table. **Serves 4***

6 tablespoons (¾ stick) unsalted butter
2 pounds yellow onions, halved and thinly sliced
Leaves from 2 large sprigs fresh thyme, chopped
1 bay leaf
1 tablespoon all-purpose flour
½ teaspoon kosher salt
1 teaspoon freshly ground black pepper
1 cup dry white wine
4 cups beef broth
2 cups water
Four ½-inch-thick slices of French bread
½ pound Gruyère cheese, shredded

1. In a large heavy pot over medium heat, melt the butter. Add the onions, thyme, and bay leaf. Cook for about 40 minutes, stirring often, until the onions are caramelized and soft.
2. Stir in the flour, salt, and pepper and cook for 1 minute. Add the wine and continue to cook, stirring, for 1 minute more. Add the broth and water and bring to a boil. Reduce the heat to a simmer and cook, uncovered, for 20 to 30 minutes, until the flavors saturate the soup. Taste and add salt and pepper if needed.
3. While the soup cooks, preheat the oven to 375°F.

4. Toast the baguette slices on a baking sheet in the oven, turning them after about 6 minutes. Remove them from the oven as soon as they are golden brown. Set the oven to broil.

5. Remove and discard the bay leaf, and ladle the soup into ovenproof crocks or bowls. Place one of the toast slices on the top of each bowl of soup, and cover the bread and soup with a thick layer of the shredded cheese. Broil for about 1 minute, watching closely to ensure the cheese is melted and bubbling but not burnt. Serve hot.

SPLIT PEA **SOUP**

This hearty soup makes good use of ham bones—it's often made right after Easter and other holiday celebrations as a way to use the leftover bone. You can also buy ham bones from a butcher, or substitute smoked ham hocks, which can usually be found at large grocery stores. The point is to add a bit of pork saltiness and sturdy character to the soup, to supplement the smooth, broken-down peas. We use a few basic spices to prevent the soup from being boring, but it doesn't need a lot to be substantial and gratifying. Follow the instructions for cooking time, but you'll really know the soup is done by its velvety texture. ***Serves 4 to 6***

2 tablespoons unsalted butter

1 yellow onion, chopped

1 carrot, peeled and diced

1 cup chopped ham

1 ham bone or smoked ham hock

One 16-ounce package green split peas

1 large bay leaf

3 sprigs fresh thyme

Dash of ground allspice

1 teaspoon kosher salt

$\frac{1}{2}$ teaspoon freshly ground black pepper

1. In a 6-quart or larger pot over medium heat, melt the butter. Add the onion, carrot, and ham and cook for about 5 minutes, or until the onion and ham begin to brown.
2. Add the ham bone and 8 cups cold water. Add the split peas, bay leaf, thyme, allspice, salt, and pepper and bring to a boil. Reduce the heat to a simmer and cook, stirring occasionally, until the peas are entirely soft and falling apart, about 2 to 2½ hours.
3. Remove and discard the ham bone, bay leaf, and thyme sprigs. Taste the soup and add additional salt and pepper as necessary. Serve hot.

TOMATO SOUP **AND** GRILLED CHEESE SANDWICHES

Certain classics define comfort food. These are the reassuring, filling meals that we all remember from childhood, uncomplicated culinary gems that our mothers set before us as tokens of love. At the top of that particular list sits a silky tomato soup partnered with the crunchy, melty, salty goodness of a perfectly grilled cheese sandwich. The combo is best served when the rain is coming down in sheets, or it is way too cold to be outside. But as far as any kid is concerned, this soup is just as good on sunny days.

Serves 4

SOUP

3 tablespoons extra-virgin olive oil

1 tablespoon unsalted butter

1 yellow onion, diced

1 large garlic clove, smashed and peeled

2 tablespoons all-purpose flour

2½ cups low-sodium chicken broth

One 28-ounce can diced San Marzano plum tomatoes, with the juice

2 tablespoons tomato paste

1 tablespoon sugar

1 teaspoon chopped fresh thyme leaves

Kosher salt and freshly ground black pepper

SANDWICHES

8 slices sourdough bread (or your favorite thick-sliced sandwich bread)

4 tablespoons (½ stick) unsalted butter, softened

8 to 12 slices cheddar cheese

1. Make the soup: Heat the olive oil and butter in a 6-quart nonreactive pot over medium-high heat until the butter melts. Add the onion and garlic and sauté until softened but not browned.

2. Add the flour and stir until the onion is evenly coated. Add the broth, tomatoes with their juices, tomato paste, sugar, and thyme. Season lightly with salt and pepper, and stir the soup until it comes to a simmer. Lower the heat to medium-low, cover, and cook for 40 minutes. Check the soup often and adjust the temperature as needed to keep it at a gentle simmer.

3. Puree the soup in batches in a blender (or use an immersion blender to puree it all at once). Transfer the pureed soup to a large bowl until you've processed all of it, then return it to the pot and keep warm over low heat while you make the grilled cheese sandwiches.

4. Make the sandwiches: Heat a heavy skillet over medium heat. Butter one side of all the bread slices, making sure the butter is applied evenly.

5. Sandwich 2 or 3 slices of the cheese between 2 slices of bread, with the buttered sides out. Toast in the skillet, checking often to ensure the bread is not burning. Flip the sandwiches as soon as the bottoms are golden brown. When both sides are browned and the cheese has melted, transfer to a cutting board.

6. Let the sandwiches sit for 2 minutes before slicing each one on the diagonal. Serve with a bowl of the hot soup.

CREAM OF MUSHROOM SOUP

This recipe is a canvas on which to paint your own flavors. Both the cream base and the mushrooms are amazingly adaptable to other flavors, from hot sauce to oregano. So play with the recipe and add a pinch here and a pinch there. Or really change things up by using a mix of different wild mushrooms or even adding a little shaved truffle or truffle oil. No matter what, this soup is sure to be an unexpected delight on the dinner table. ***Serves 4***

    2 tablespoons extra-virgin olive oil
    2 tablespoons unsalted butter
    1 yellow onion, finely diced
    2 garlic cloves, chopped
    1 pound brown button mushrooms, cleaned, stems trimmed
    2 tablespoons all-purpose flour
    ½ cup dry white wine
    3 cups chicken broth
    2 large sprigs fresh thyme
    1½ cups heavy cream
    Kosher salt and freshly ground black pepper
    2 tablespoons chopped fresh flat-leaf parsley

1. In a large pot over medium-high heat, heat the olive oil and butter until the butter melts.
2. Add the onion and garlic and cook until the onion has softened, 6 to 8 minutes. Add the mushrooms and stir to thoroughly combine. Cook, stirring frequently, until the mushrooms are soft and starting to take on color, 10 to 12 minutes.
3. Sprinkle the flour over the mushrooms and stir until the mushrooms are completely coated. Add the wine and deglaze the pan, scraping up any browned bits from the bottom.
4. Add the broth and thyme and bring to a boil. Reduce the heat to a simmer and cook until the liquid has reduced by one-quarter, about 15 minutes.
5. Stir in the cream, taste, and season with salt and pepper as needed. Bring to a simmer and cook for about 3 minutes, or until heated through.

6. Working in batches, transfer the soup to a blender and blend on high for 10 seconds, then transfer to a large bowl. When you've blended all the soup, return it to the pot and reheat over medium heat for 2 minutes. Serve hot, sprinkled with the parsley.

BLUE **BLOODS** KITCHEN **TIP**

The mushrooms in this soup, like mushrooms in any recipe, should be cleaned thoroughly before cooking. However, never rinse mushrooms—they absorb water like a sponge and that will prevent them from browning properly. Excess moisture can also lead to a rubbery texture. Instead, brush the mushrooms clean with a slightly damp paper towel, or a clean, soft-bristled toothbrush. (You can even buy a special mushroom-cleaning brush at high-end kitchen supply stores, but that's not something you would find in the Reagans' kitchen!)

MANHATTAN CLAM CHOWDER

There are only two types of clam chowder that matter in the world—New England and Manhattan. But when you're filming the police commissioner of New York City, there's only one choice that makes any sense. With a lighter tomato base and a smattering of fresh vegetables perfectly cooked, this clam chowder is the ideal starter to a multi-course meal. That said, it still holds up well as a meal in a bowl after a long chilly night shift in the City that Never Sleeps. **Serves 4**

3 tablespoons canola oil

1 yellow onion, diced

2 garlic cloves, minced

2 carrots, peeled and chopped

2 celery stalks, chopped

3 sprigs fresh thyme

1/4 teaspoon celery seed

1 bay leaf

Kosher salt and freshly ground black pepper

1 tablespoon tomato paste

One 14.5-ounce can crushed tomatoes

Two 8-ounce bottles clam juice

Two 10-ounce cans baby clams, juice reserved

1 pound Yukon Gold or fingerling potatoes, peeled and cubed

1. In a large pot over medium-high heat, heat the oil. Add the onion and garlic and cook until slightly soft, about 3 minutes.
2. Add the carrots and celery and cook until the celery begins to soften, about 5 minutes. Add the thyme, celery seed, and bay leaf and season with salt and pepper. Stir and cook for about 2 minutes. Add the tomato paste, stir thoroughly to incorporate, and cook for 1 minute.
3. Add the tomatoes, bottled clam juice, the reserved juice from the canned clams, and the potatoes. Stir to mix well. Reduce the heat to a simmer, cover, and simmer for 40 to 45 minutes until the potatoes are fork-tender.
4. Remove and discard the thyme sprigs and bay leaf. Add the canned clams and cook for 5 minutes. Serve hot.

COURTESY OF . . . **WILL ESTES**

Will Estes plays the youngest Reagan brother, Jamie, on the show. Will is an incredibly sweet soul, devoted to animal charities. He's also a vegetarian. During the family dinner scene, he keeps a vegetable smoothie under his chair because he usually can't eat most of what's served for the scene. As wonderful as he is, Will is not what you would call an accomplished cook. When he offered this healthy alternative for the book, we decided to include it . . . with a warning: getting it down will be far more challenging than preparing it (the title pretty much says it all).

THE GET-IT-OVER-WITH RAW GREEN GAZPACHO
   1 carrot, peeled
   1 celery stalk
   1 cucumber, peeled and chopped
   1 to 3 garlic cloves (depending on your courage, and who you might kiss)
   1 small bunch fresh cilantro, stems trimmed
   $\frac{1}{2}$ jalapeño pepper
   1 handful fresh spinach
   1 to 3 large leaves Swiss chard (or substitute kale or dandelion leaves)
   Juice of $\frac{1}{2}$ lemon (optional)
   3 tablespoons olive oil

Combine all the ingredients in a powerful blender or juicer and blend until smooth. You can play with different ingredients and dial back the strength by reducing the amount of garlic or jalapeño in the "soup."

POTATO-LEEK SOUP

As anyone from a true Irish family can tell you, potatoes on their own can become a little bit dull. Combining plain old spuds with a rich but subtle onion flavor courtesy of the vegetable emblem of Wales is a wonderful way to make a filling and elegant soup. We've used waxy yellow potatoes, which add silkiness without competing with the leek's distinctive taste. A healthy dose of buttermilk adds bite and brings all the other flavors together. ***Serves 4***

2 tablespoons unsalted butter

1 tablespoon canola oil

2 large leeks (white parts only), sliced and cleaned

Kosher salt

1 pound Yukon Gold or similar potatoes, peeled and cubed

2 cups chicken broth,

3/4 cup heavy cream

1/2 cup buttermilk

1/2 teaspoon white pepper

1 tablespoon finely chopped fresh flat-leaf parsley

1. In a large pot over medium-high heat, combine the butter and canola oil and heat until the butter has melted. Add the leeks and reduce the heat to medium-low. Season with salt and cook until the leeks begin to soften, 10 to 15 minutes.
2. Add the potatoes and broth, increase the heat to high, and bring to a boil. Reduce the heat to low, cover, and simmer until the potatoes are tender, about 35 minutes.
3. Working in batches, transfer the soup to a blender and blend until completely smooth. Transfer the blended soup to a large bowl. When all the soup is blended, return it to the pot and reheat over medium-low heat.
4. Whisk in the cream, buttermilk, and white pepper. Taste and add additional salt and pepper as needed. Serve hot in individual bowls, sprinkled with the parsley.

CHICKEN NOODLE SOUP

This lovely soup will cure all that ails you—or at the very least, take care of serious hunger pangs! Its simple salty flavor can satisfy the loudest growl in your stomach without making you feel overly full. An unexpected burst of lemon brightens the soup and makes it as appropriate for a spring evening on the patio as it is for hunkering down inside in the colder months. The noodles are the one nod to decadence in a good-for-you soup. Serve it steaming hot so the vapors can whet your appetite. Partner it with a sturdy bread, like the Irish Soda Bread on page 197, to soak up every last drop of that savory broth. **Serves 4**

1 teaspoon canola oil
1 yellow onion, finely diced
2 garlic cloves, minced
2 celery stalks, finely diced
1 carrot, peeled and finely diced
1 teaspoon lemon pepper seasoning
6 cups low-sodium chicken stock
8 ounces egg noodles
Kosher salt and freshly ground black pepper
1 tablespoon finely chopped fresh flat-leaf parsley
Finely grated zest of 1 lemon

1. In a large pot over medium-high heat, heat the oil. Add the onion and garlic and cook until the onion softens, about 3 minutes.
2. Add the celery, carrot, and lemon pepper and cook, stirring, for 1 minute. Add the chicken stock and bring to a boil. Reduce the heat to a simmer and cook for 10 minutes.
3. Add the noodles and simmer for 5 minutes, or until the noodles are cooked through. Taste the soup and season with the salt and black pepper as needed.
4. Top the soup with the parsley. Transfer to individual bowls and sprinkle with lemon zest before serving.

YANKEE BEAN SOUP

This is a New England favorite, revered for the sturdy nature of the Great Northern beans and luscious texture of the finished soup. It was invented for nights when the rain is blowing sideways and everyone at the table has been chilled to the bone. From the very first spoonful, the weather outside will be forgotten, and all attention will turn to the kitchen and a concern that there may not be enough left in the pot for seconds.

Serves 4 to 6

1 pound dried Great Northern beans, rinsed and drained
1 teaspoon canola oil
1 cup diced bacon (about 4 thick-cut slices)
3 garlic cloves, minced
1 yellow onion, chopped
1 teaspoon dried thyme
Pinch of cayenne pepper
¼ teaspoon white pepper
¼ cup pure maple syrup
¼ cup ketchup
1 tablespoon Worcestershire sauce
2 teaspoons ground mustard
4 cups boiling water
1 bay leaf
Kosher salt and freshly ground black pepper

1. In a large saucepan, combine the beans with enough water to cover by 1 inch and bring to a boil over high heat. Boil for 5 minutes.
2. Remove the pan from the heat, cover, and set aside for 1 hour.
3. Drain and rinse the beans. In a large pot or Dutch oven, heat the oil over medium–high heat. Add the bacon and cook just until it browns, about 3 minutes. Add the garlic and onion and cook until the onion is soft and starting to brown.
4. Add the thyme, cayenne, and white pepper and cook, stirring, for 1 minute. Add the maple syrup, ketchup, Worcestershire sauce, and mustard and cook, stirring, for 1 minute more.

5. Add the drained beans to the pot, along with the 4 cups boiling water and bay leaf, and bring to a boil. Reduce to a simmer, cover, and cook until the beans are completely tender, about 1½ hours. Remove and discard the bay leaf.
6. Taste the soup and season with salt and black pepper as needed. Serve warm.

ON THE SET . . . **WITH BRIDGET**

Donnie Wahlberg is one of my best buds from way back, and an incredibly fun actor to have on set. We are constantly amazed at the amount of food he puts away during shooting and even between takes—all without gaining weight. But the best part of having him at the Reagans' family dinner table is the comic relief. The truth is, Donnie plays with his food. The kids at the table can't wait for that moment between takes when Donnie sticks green beans or some other food up under his lip and makes a goofy fang face. To be honest, some of the adults look forward to it as well.

BLACK BEAN SOUP

The secret to this surprisingly zesty soup are the many Mediterranean touches that give it a smoky, spicy, and delightfully interesting twist. Black beans are always a sturdy and, when blended, silky stage on which other flavors just seem to shine. We have been careful not to overdo the accents in this recipe; the spiciness is more varied than actually hot. Still, you won't find a more captivating use for black beans in your house. We use canned, although if you're willing to wait a few hours while dried beans soak, you can save a little bit of money by using dried beans. **Serves 4**

1 tablespoon extra-virgin olive oil
1 white onion, diced
3 garlic cloves, minced
1 teaspoon chili powder
1 tablespoon dried oregano
1/2 teaspoon smoked paprika
1 teaspoon ground cumin
Kosher salt and freshly ground black pepper
Three 15-ounce cans black beans, drained but not rinsed
2 1/2 cups cold water
1 bay leaf
1 tablespoon chopped fresh cilantro
1/4 cup sour cream or plain yogurt (optional)

1. In a large pot, heat the olive oil over medium-high heat. Add the onion and garlic and stir until the onion has softened, about 3 minutes.
2. Add the chili powder, oregano, paprika, and cumin and stir until the onion is evenly coated. Season liberally with salt and pepper and cook for 1 minute.
3. Add the black beans and stir to thoroughly mix. Cook for 2 minutes.
4. Add the cold water and the bay leaf and bring to a boil. Reduce the heat and gently simmer for 30 minutes.
5. Transfer half the soup to a blender and blend on high for about 5 seconds, or until the soup is smooth. Return the blended soup to the pot. Stir in the cilantro and serve the soup hot, garnished with sour cream or plain yogurt, if desired.

SALADS

SIMPLE THREE-LETTUCE DINNER SALAD

If you're putting a heavy meal (like just about every Blue Bloods' *family dinner) on the family dinner table, a basic fresh salad with bright flavors, a variety of fresh greens, and a light dressing is a must. Let's be clear here: that doesn't mean the salad should be uninteresting. Boring is the cardinal sin among salads, and this easy-to-assemble recipe is anything but. The combination of lettuces mixes a little bitter, a touch of sweet, and a lot of crunch. An elegant lemon vinaigrette puts the salad over the top. You may want to make more of the vinaigrette and refrigerate it to use on other salads, or even fish.*
Serves 4

SALAD

    1 small head radicchio
    1 small head endive
    1 large head butter lettuce

VINAIGRETTE

    3 tablespoons extra-virgin olive oil
    1 tablespoon champagne vinegar
    1 tablespoon fresh lemon juice
    1 teaspoon sugar
    1 small shallot, minced
    Kosher salt and freshly ground black pepper

1. Prepare the salad greens: Trim and remove the stem ends of each of the lettuces. Tear the leaves into pieces all roughly the same size. Wash, dry, and combine in a large salad bowl.
2. Make the vinaigrette: Combine the olive oil, vinegar, lemon juice, sugar, and shallot in a small bowl and whisk until emulsified. Taste and season with salt and pepper as needed.
3. Drizzle the vinaigrette over the salad, toss to coat, and serve.

FRESH CORN-**AND**-PEPPER **SALAD**

*Everyone should have an easy summer salad in their arsenal, one that exploits the best of the seasonal produce available. This is just about the best we've come across. If sunshine had a flavor, it would be the tart citrus notes in this wonderful salad. Make it in summer with the finest produce you can find at the local farmers' market or upscale grocery store, and the salad will scream "fresh." Or, if you have a hankering during the colder months, you can just as easily substitute canned corn for the corn on the cob. Either way, the salad will wake up your taste buds and cut the heaviness of steak, burgers, or other meat dishes. **Serves 4 to 6**

SALAD
4 ears corn, shucked and cleaned
1 small red onion, finely diced
1 large red bell pepper, seeded and diced

DRESSING
1 tablespoon apple cider vinegar
2 tablespoons fresh lemon juice
$1/3$ cup extra-virgin olive oil
$1/2$ teaspoon kosher salt
$1/2$ teaspoon freshly ground black pepper

$1/2$ cup julienned fresh basil leaves

1. Make the salad: Fill a large pot with 3 to 4 quarts water, salt it heavily, and bring to a boil. Fill a large bowl with a mixture of half ice and half cold water.
2. Break the ears of corn in half, add them to the pot, and boil for about 3 minutes. The kernels should be bright yellow but not withered. Transfer the corn to the ice water bath and let cool completely.
3. Cut the kernels off each cob by holding the cob on end on a cutting board and slicing down close to the cob. Put the kernels in a large bowl. Add the onion and bell pepper to the bowl and stir to combine.

4. Make the dressing: In a small bowl, combine the vinegar, lemon juice, olive oil, salt, and black pepper and whisk until emulsified. Pour the dressing over the salad and mix well until all the vegetables are coated. Top with the basil and stir again to mix it in.

5. Refrigerate the salad for at least 30 minutes, or up to 2 hours. Remove from the refrigerator and allow to come to room temperature before serving to allow the flavors to bloom. Taste before serving, and add salt and black pepper as needed.

SALAD NIÇOISE

A French sidewalk café masterpiece, salade niçoise is meant to be an elegant, light, meal-in-one. It is traditionally a simple lunch that doesn't slow you down. This version can serve the same role, but we've cut back on the amount of tuna so that you can also use it as the starter for a main course. If you prefer a more substantial salad, substitute the freshest tuna you can buy (sushi quality), and just sear it on the outside so that it is still pink in the middle—then slice it thinly and top each salad with two or three slices.

Serves 4

VINAIGRETTE

1 large shallot, minced

1 tablespoon capers, drained

1 tablespoon Dijon mustard

2 tablespoons champagne vinegar

$1/2$ teaspoon kosher salt

Freshly ground black pepper

$1/4$ cup extra-virgin olive oil

SALAD

$1/2$ pound haricots verts, ends trimmed (or substitute small fresh green beans)

1 pound small red potatoes

4 large eggs

1 pint cherry tomatoes, halved

4 radishes, thinly sliced

4 ounces kalamata olives, pitted

2 tablespoons chopped fresh chives

8 to 12 anchovies (optional)

Two 6-ounce cans water-packed solid white tuna, drained

1. Make the vinaigrette: In a small bowl, whisk together the shallot, capers, mustard, vinegar, salt, and pepper. Add the oil in a thin stream, whisking constantly until the vinaigrette is emulsified.

2. Make the salad: Fill a large pot three-quarters full of water, salt it heavily, and bring to a boil. Fill a large heatproof bowl with a mixture of half ice and half cold water.

3. Boil the beans for 2 minutes, drain, and plunge into the ice water bath. Once the beans are cool, drain them. Cut the beans in half diagonally.

4. Put the potatoes into the pot and cover with cold water. Salt lightly and bring a boil over high heat. Reduce to a simmer and cook until tender, 12 to 15 minutes. Drain the potatoes and set aside to cool. When the potatoes are cool, cut them in half (or quarter them, if large).

5. In a small pot, cover the eggs with cold water and bring to a boil over high heat. Remove from the heat, cover, and set aside for 15 minutes.

6. Rinse the eggs under cold water until cooled. Peel and cut in half lengthwise.

7. In a large bowl, combine the beans, potatoes, tomatoes, radishes, olives, and chives. Pour three-quarters of the vinaigrette over the salad and toss until well coated.

8. Arrange the salad on four individual salad plates. Put an egg half on the side of each plate. Arrange the anchovies on each salad (if using), and top each with one-quarter of the tuna. Drizzle the remaining vinaigrette over the top and serve.

BAKED GOAT CHEESE SALAD

Simplicity is never so delectable as when it is Mediterranean simplicity. Lightly breaded goat cheese is the small decadence in a salad that would be right at home in a coastal Greek villa. Don't worry about the cheese—this creation is otherwise purely heart healthy and spilling over with freshness. These are salad flavors at their best, but the appeal doesn't stop at the flavors. The intriguing contrast of crunchy, soft, and creamy makes this a crowd-pleaser for lunch, or a great, light way to start off a family meal.

Serves 4

 $\frac{1}{4}$ cup pine nuts
 One 4-ounce log goat cheese
 $\frac{1}{4}$ cup panko bread crumbs
 $\frac{1}{2}$ cup extra-virgin olive oil
 2 tablespoons fresh lemon juice
 1 tablespoon minced shallot
 1 teaspoon Dijon mustard
 Kosher salt and freshly ground black pepper
 2 cups baby spinach, washed and dried
 2 cups arugula, washed and dried

1. Preheat the oven to 450°F.
2. In a small saucepan over medium–high heat, toast the pine nuts until they begin to brown. Set aside.
3. Cut the goat cheese crosswise into 4 equal-size medallions. Place the bread crumbs in one small bowl and 1 tablespoon of the olive oil in a second small bowl.
4. Dip a goat cheese medallion into the olive oil, so that it is lightly coated all over. Allow any extra oil to drip off. Press and roll the medallion in the bread crumbs until it is evenly coated on all sides. Place the medallion on a baking sheet. Repeat with the rest of the medallions.
5. Bake the goat cheese for 2 to 3 minutes, or until the bread crumbs turn light golden brown.

6. While the cheese is baking, combine the remaining olive oil, lemon juice, shallot, and mustard in a small bowl and whisk until emulsified. Taste and season with salt and pepper as needed.

7. In a large salad bowl, combine the spinach and arugula and toss to mix. Drizzle the dressing over the greens and toss until they are evenly coated.

8. Divide the dressed greens among four large salad plates. Place a baked goat cheese medallion on each plate, centered on the greens. Sprinkle with the toasted pine nuts and serve.

SUPER-SIMPLE MACARONI SALAD

Yes, super simple, but also super good. This cookout favorite has no pretensions, and it goes wonderfully with main courses from burgers to fried chicken. Best of all, the salad can be adapted in any number of ways to suit you or your family's preferences. Add shallots or chives for a bit more oniony bite, or choose a rainbow of bell pepper colors to add some visual zing. If you're a carrot fan, grated carrots work wonderfully with the other flavors in this salad. You can also dress up this creamy delight with just about any herb you can name. It's even the perfect stage for Roasted Garlic (page 250)!

Serves 4 to 6

$^3/_4$ cup real mayonnaise

$^1/_4$ cup sour cream

2 teaspoons Dijon mustard

1 teaspoon Worcestershire sauce

1 tablespoon fresh lemon juice

$^1/_2$ teaspoon kosher salt

$^1/_2$ teaspoon freshly ground black pepper

4 cups cooked elbow macaroni, rinsed and drained

$^1/_3$ cup diced red bell pepper

$^1/_2$ cup diced celery

$^1/_3$ cup finely diced red onion

1 tablespoon capers, drained

1. In a large bowl, combine the mayonnaise, sour cream, mustard, Worcestershire sauce, and lemon juice. Whisk until completely mixed. Add the salt and black pepper and whisk until incorporated.
2. Add the macaroni and stir until completely coated. Add the bell pepper, celery, onion, and capers. Stir until all the ingredients are evenly distributed.
3. Refrigerate the salad for at least 1 hour and up to overnight. Prior to serving, taste and add salt and black pepper as needed.

ON THE SET . . . **WITH BRIDGET**

I can't imagine anybody being less of a salad lover than Tom Selleck. I sit next to him during the family dinner scene, and he reminds me a lot of my dad: he likes meat, meat, and more meat. A garnish is as much a vegetable or salad course as he ever wants to see on his plate. Knowing how much he hates vegetables, I find it really funny that he actually owns a large avocado farm in Los Angeles. I'm just waiting for the day when he announces that he's fed up with all that green, and that he's turned it into a cattle ranch.

PICNIC POTATO SALAD

What would a picnic be without a hearty potato salad? Although it is substantial enough to squash hunger pangs, this version of the cookout standard keeps things a little bit lighter than usual, omitting the traditional egg, and cutting back on the mayonnaise. Of course, the secret to any great potato salad is to slip in some fresh crunch to cut the heaviness of the all-purpose tuber. You don't have to rely on the celery in this version—you can swap in diced fennel or jicama for a slightly more exotic edge. **Serves 4**

3 pounds Russet potatoes, peeled
1 tablespoon table salt
2 tablespoons apple cider vinegar
1 cup real mayonnaise
$1/4$ cup buttermilk
3 tablespoons Dijon mustard
$1/2$ cup chopped fresh dill
Dash of smoked paprika
Kosher salt and freshly ground black pepper
$3/4$ cup diced celery
$1/2$ cup diced red onion
$1/2$ cup diced red bell pepper
2 tablespoons capers, drained

1. Put the potatoes in a large pot and cover with cold water. Bring to a boil over high heat and add the table salt. Boil the potatoes for 15 minutes or until fork-tender. When the potatoes are done, drain in a colander. Set aside until cool enough to handle.
2. Dice the potatoes while still warm, and transfer to a large bowl. Sprinkle them with the vinegar and gently mix until they are evenly coated with the vinegar.
3. In a small bowl, combine the mayonnaise, buttermilk, mustard, dill, and paprika and stir until incorporated. Taste and season with kosher salt and black pepper as needed.
4. Pour the dressing over the potatoes and gently mix to coat, being careful not to break up the potatoes.
5. Add the celery, onion, bell pepper, and capers and gently stir until well mixed. Refrigerate the salad, covered, for at least 1 hour before serving.

CLASSIC WALDORF SALAD

The story goes that this salad was created by the maître d'hôtel at the Waldorf Hotel (before it merged and became the world-famous icon, the Waldorf-Astoria). Hoping to create a surprisingly sweet and refreshing summer lunch salad, Oscar Tschirky combined apples, grapes, sour cream, and lettuce in a truly unique creation. The salad has evolved over time to include walnuts, but it's still all about that super-fresh crunch and surprising sweetness. This is rarely used as a starter—it's basically a meal-in-one. Serve it to the kids at the table and watch the smiles bloom. (Spoiler alert: The adults will probably want in on the action!) Serves 4

½ cup walnut halves

½ cup sour cream

3 tablespoons real mayonnaise

2 tablespoons chopped fresh flat-leaf parsley

1 teaspoon honey

Finely grated zest and juice of 1 lemon

Freshly ground black pepper

1 large Red Delicious apple

1 large Granny Smith apple

2 small celery stalks, chopped

¼ cup raisins

½ cup halved seedless red grapes

1 large head butter lettuce, trimmed, washed, and dried

1. Preheat the oven to 350°F.
2. Spread out the walnuts on a baking sheet. Toast in the oven for 10 minutes. Cool and coarsely chop the nuts.
3. In a large bowl, combine the sour cream, mayonnaise, parsley, honey, and lemon zest. Season lightly with pepper and whisk until completely mixed.
4. Halve and core the apples. Cut into slices lengthwise and cut the slices into

thirds. Add the apples, celery, raisins, and grapes to the bowl with the dressing. Drizzle with the lemon juice and toss to coat. Cover and refrigerate the salad if not serving immediately.

5. To serve, tear the lettuce into bite-size pieces. Place the lettuce in a wide, shallow salad bowl or on a serving platter. Spread the apple mixture over the lettuce, top with the toasted walnuts, and serve.

THREE-BEAN SALAD

The challenge with a bean salad is to keep the dish from becoming too heavy. We answered that challenge by using a perfect combination of creamy and crunchy beans along with a sparkling dressing that gives the beans a slight, pleasantly acidic edge. It's an addictive flavor that will make the salad disappear. But put it on the table early because you'll want to impress everyone with the stunning color combinations. This is a confetti mix of hues and shapes that looks like art in the bowl and eats like the salad equivalent of candy. **Serves 4**

½ pound haricots verts, trimmed and cut on the diagonal into thirds
One 15-ounce can garbanzo beans, drained and rinsed
One 15-ounce can kidney beans, drained and rinsed
½ red onion, finely chopped
3 tablespoons sugar (or substitute honey)
⅓ cup fresh lemon juice
¼ cup canola oil
¾ teaspoon kosher salt
¼ teaspoon freshly ground black pepper
1 tablespoon chopped fresh chives

1. Fill a large pot with water, salt it heavily, and bring to a boil. Fill a large heatproof bowl with a mixture of half ice and half cold water.
2. Add the haricots verts to the boiling water and blanch for about 1 minute, or until bright green and just tender. Drain and transfer the beans to the ice water bath. Once cooled, drain and let the beans dry.
3. In a large bowl, combine all the beans with the onion and toss to mix.
4. In a small saucepan, over medium heat, combine the sugar, lemon juice, oil, salt, and pepper. Bring to a simmer and remove from the heat. Pour over the beans.
5. Let the salad sit at room temperature for about 1 hour, tossing regularly to coat. When ready to serve, top with the chives.

BLUE **BLOODS** KITCHEN **TIP**

Although the fresh haricots verts in this bean salad provide a lot of crunch, you can save time and energy by replacing them with one 15-ounce can sliced green beans, drained. This is also the best option if you can't find haricots verts or fresh green beans in your area.

VEGETARIAN COUSCOUS SALAD

Follow the coastline of the Mediterranean and you'll take a tour of the brightest, most sparkling flavors used in the kitchen. We've taken advantage of those flavors in this elegant salad bursting with freshness. A light vinegar, a kiss of citrus, and a drizzle of high-quality olive oil make for a barely there dressing that allows all the other flavors to shine through. The crunch of the vegetables contrasts with the pleasingly fine-textured couscous, and creates a memorable, airy summer meal. Serve this for the vegetarians at the table, or any time you're hankering for a refreshing meal that will completely satisfy your hunger without making you feel full. **Serves 4 to 6**

COUSCOUS SALAD

1 large red bell pepper

1 large orange bell pepper

One 10-ounce box couscous, cooked according to package directions

1 large cucumber, peeled, halved lengthwise, seeded, and sliced

1 small red onion, diced

1/3 cup chopped fresh flat-leaf parsley

1/2 cup chopped fresh cilantro

DRESSING

2 tablespoons white wine vinegar

2 tablespoons fresh lemon juice

1/4 cup extra-virgin olive oil

Kosher salt and freshly ground black pepper

1 pint cherry or grape tomatoes, halved (about 2 cups)

1. Make the salad. Preheat the oven to 500°F.
2. Roast the bell peppers in the oven for 30 minutes. Transfer to a paper bag and seal tightly. Let steam in the bag for 10 to 15 minutes, or until the peppers are cool enough to handle.
3. Remove the roasted peppers from the bag and pull the skins off. Remove and discard the stems and seeds, and let cool completely. Chop the peppers.

4. In a large glass bowl, combine the cooked couscous, cucumber, onion, parsley, cilantro, and roasted peppers. Using a large fork, stir gently until well mixed.
5. Make the dressing: In a small bowl, combine the vinegar, lemon juice, and olive oil and whisk until incorporated. Taste and season with salt and black pepper as needed. Drizzle the dressing over the couscous and vegetables and stir to coat.
6. Add the tomatoes and carefully fold them into the salad without crushing. Cover and refrigerate the salad for at least 1 hour, or until you're ready to serve.

BLUE **BLOODS** KITCHEN **TIP**

Pressed for time? You can replace the homemade roasted peppers in this recipe with ½ cup jarred roasted peppers without doing any damage to the salad (although you'll lose the color of the orange bell pepper).

BEHIND THE SCENES . . . **WITH WENDY**

The actors on the *Blue Bloods'* set have watched Sami Gayle grow up. But truth be told, the young woman who plays Nicole "Nicky" Reagan-Boyle was already a show-biz pro when she started on the show at age fourteen. Sami had enjoyed a long run as Baby June in the Great White Way's production of *Gypsy*, and had just wrapped up a film role when she took the part of Nicky. As you might expect, she's a heck of a singer and dancer. Of course, she's not alone. Len Cariou, a classically trained actor who plays grandfather Henry Reagan on the show, is a Tony-award-winning Broadway legend who starred in numerous musicals including *Sweeney Todd* and *A Little Night Music*. The writers and producers really wanted to team the two up and showcase their talents in an episode, and finally managed to do it in season two, in the episode entitled "The Life We Choose." Nicky agrees to do a duet with Henry for a fund-raiser. Their duet of "I Don't Need Anything But You" from the Broadway show *Annie* is one of the most memorable moments in *Blue Bloods'* history—a case of art imitating art.

SPINACH, AVOCADO, AND ORANGE SALAD

Citrus adds immeasurably to any salad, but especially to one based on sturdy greens. The spinach bed in this salad provides the perfect foundation for succulent orange suprêmes *married to delicate slices of rich and creamy avocado. A little crunch courtesy of walnuts cuts the richness and adds some interest to the salad. Every great salad also needs a great vinaigrette, so we've used a surprising lime version to provide the salad with an eye-opening tart flavor. You can easily customize this simple creation to put your own spin on it. Try substituting blood oranges, ruby grapefruit, or Meyer lemons for the orange.* **Serves 4**

VINAIGRETTE

2 tablespoons extra-virgin olive oil

1 tablespoon fresh lime juice

2 teaspoons Dijon mustard

Kosher salt and freshly ground black pepper

SALAD

4 cups baby spinach

2 large navel oranges, cut into suprêmes (see tip, page 52)

2 tablespoons chopped walnuts

1 large firm avocado

1. Make the vinaigrette: In a small bowl, whisk together the oil, lime juice, and mustard. Taste and season with salt and pepper as needed.
2. Make the salad: In a large salad bowl, combine the spinach and orange suprêmes and toss lightly. Scatter the walnuts over the salad.
3. Drizzle the vinaigrette over the salad and toss until the spinach is coated.
4. Cut the avocado in half, remove the pit, and carefully scoop out the flesh of each half with a spoon. Cut the avocado into very thin slices, and cut all the slices in half crosswise.
5. Add the avocado to the salad and toss lightly, just until the avocado is coated with the vinaigrette. Serve immediately.

BLUE **BLOODS** KITCHEN **TIP**

Cutting *suprêmes* is a way to make citrus more attractive and to remove everything but the delicious flesh. It's not hard to do, and it's a great way to dress up any dish that includes oranges, limes, or other citrus. Start with a very sharp knife. Slice off each end of the orange (or other citrus), exposing the fruit's flesh. Sit the orange on a cutting board on one cut end. Following the curve of the fruit, carefully slice away both the peel and the bitter white pith, leaving only the flesh of the fruit. Next, slice on either side of the membrane holding each segment of fruit in place. Make each cut as close as possible to the membrane, to preserve as much of the flesh as you can. Remove the segments and you'll have beautiful, juicy tidbits ideal for salads, fruit plates, and desserts of all kinds.

COBB SALAD

*Legend has it that this salad was invented by the owner of the famed Hollywood restaurant the Brown Derby. According to the tale, owner Robert Cobb felt a bit peckish at the end of one particularly busy night. He went into the kitchen and threw together a salad with basically anything he could find in the restaurant's refrigerator that was leftover from the busy night. As apocryphal as the story might be, we know for certain that the salad has always included a meat-lover's dream combination of bacon, hard-boiled eggs, chicken, and ham. Avocados and iceberg lettuce help maintain the "salad" cred of this full meal on a plate. We like to substitute healthier Romaine, but the final choice is up to you. **Serves 4 to 6***

DRESSING
½ cup extra-virgin olive oil
2 tablespoons red wine vinegar
1 tablespoon fresh lemon juice
1 teaspoon Dijon mustard
1 teaspoon Worcestershire sauce
1 small garlic clove, minced
Kosher salt and freshly ground black pepper

SALAD
1 large head iceberg lettuce, chopped
4 ounces blue cheese, chopped
8 strips cooked bacon, chopped
3 hard-boiled eggs, peeled and cubed
2 large vine-ripened tomatoes, seeded and cubed
One 6-ounce cooked boneless, skinless, chicken breast, cubed, cut into strips or shredded, as you prefer
¼ pound ham steak, cubed
1 large avocado, pitted, peeled, and cubed

1. Make the dressing: In a small bowl, combine all the ingredients for the dressing, except for the salt and pepper, and whisk to incorporate. Taste and season with salt and pepper as needed.
2. Assemble the salad: In a large bowl, combine the lettuce with half the dressing and toss to coat.
3. Spread the lettuce out evenly across a large shallow serving bowl or platter. Divide the remaining salad ingredients in even rows on top of the lettuce. Drizzle the remaining dressing over the top and serve.

CAESAR SALAD

Here's yet another salad that comes complete with its own backstory. Credit for the salad goes to Caesar Cardini, a restaurant owner who, in the 1920s, whipped up a basic but amazingly tasty salad to make up for a depleted pantry during a Fourth of July dinner rush. It became an instant hit, adored for the compelling combination of delectable crunch and satisfyingly salty flavors. Our version forgoes the raw egg in the original. With all the other flavors, you're not likely to miss it. The anchovies add a rich, savory goodness all their own, but the original Caesar salad didn't include them, so you don't have to either (we'll understand). **Serves 4**

DRESSING

3 anchovy fillets
2 tablespoons Dijon mustard
1½ tablespoons champagne vinegar
1½ teaspoons Worcestershire sauce
1 large garlic clove, minced
Juice of ½ large lemon
½ cup extra-virgin olive oil

¼ cup grated Parmesan cheese
Freshly ground black pepper

SALAD

1 large head romaine lettuce
1 cup seasoned croutons
2 tablespoons shredded Parmesan cheese

1. Make the dressing: In the bowl of a food processor, combine the anchovies, mustard, vinegar, Worcestershire sauce, garlic, and lemon juice. Pulse until incorporated, scraping down the sides of the bowl as necessary.
2. With the food processor running, add the olive oil in a slow stream. Run the processor until the dressing has emulsified.
3. Add the grated Parmesan and pepper to taste, and pulse until incorporated. Transfer to a small bowl, cover, and refrigerate for at least 1 hour and up to overnight.
4. Assemble the salad: Trim the base of the romaine and separate the leaves. Reserve the outer leaves for another use or discard. Wash and dry the leaves of the heart.
5. Divide the romaine heart leaves among four large salad plates. Drizzle with the dressing. Scatter croutons and sprinkle some of the shredded Parmesan over each plate. Serve any leftover dressing on the side.

BARBECUE-PERFECT COLESLAW

Ask ten Southern barbecue fans the best way to make coleslaw and you're sure to get at least ten answers. That's because cabbage is just about the perfect canvas on which to paint flavors, so people like to do their own painting. To make our coleslaw stand out a bit, we throw in a small amount of red cabbage. It not only brings a subtly different flavor from green cabbage, but it also makes the salad a lot more beautiful. The rest of the ingredients are fairly basic—it's how they combine that makes them special. For a slightly more country version, substitute grainy mustard for the Dijon. **Serves 6 to 8**

1 small head green cabbage, cored and shredded
1/4 small head red cabbage, cored and shredded
1 carrot, peeled and shredded
1/4 cup apple cider vinegar
2 tablespoons sugar
1 teaspoon celery seed
2 teaspoons ground mustard
2 tablespoons Dijon mustard
1 teaspoon kosher salt
1/2 teaspoon freshly ground black pepper
1 cup real mayonnaise

1. In a large salad bowl, combine the cabbages and carrot. Toss until thoroughly mixed.
2. In a small bowl, combine the vinegar, sugar, celery seed, ground mustard, Dijon mustard, salt, and pepper and whisk until the sugar has completely dissolved and the dressing has emulsified. Add the mayonnaise and whisk until the dressing is a uniform color and texture.
3. Drizzle the dressing over the slaw one-quarter at a time. Toss and add more dressing. When you have used all the dressing, toss again until the cabbage is completely coated. Taste and add additional salt and pepper as needed.
4. Refrigerate the coleslaw for at least 3 hours and up to overnight. Remove and wait for about 10 minutes before serving, to allow the flavors to bloom.

SALAD CAPRESE

*It's amazing what Italian cooks have accomplished using a few basic ingredients in just the right combinations. Sun-kissed fresh tomatoes, quality mozzarella made with buffalo's milk, basil from the garden, and the best olive oil available may not seem like the most creative components ever gathered, but combined correctly, they translate to an otherworldly creation that is so much more than just a salad. Two bites can sweep you away to a drowsy resort on the coast of Calabria—or maybe just make for a very pleasant summer evening in the backyard. Seek out the freshest ingredients you can for this one—including ripe, organic, local tomatoes—because each part of the salad plays a critical role in making it the simple masterpiece it was meant to be. **Serves 4**

1½ pounds large vine-ripened or beefsteak tomatoes
1 pound fresh buffalo's-milk mozzarella
1 large bunch fresh basil
⅓ cup extra-virgin olive oil
Kosher salt and freshly ground black pepper

1. Cut the tomatoes and mozzarella into ¼-inch slices.
2. On a serving platter, layer a tomato slice, a large basil leaf (or 2 small leaves), and a slice of mozzarella. Repeat until all the tomatoes and mozzarella are used.
3. Drizzle with the olive oil. Season liberally with salt and pepper and serve.

APPETIZERS

SWEDISH MEATBALLS

*This is a Moynahan family favorite, and the traditional Christmas Eve recipe in Bridget's house. The Moynahans make a double (and sometimes, even a triple) batch to ensure that there are seconds and plenty of leftovers, because everyone wants to take some home (it also freezes well). It's such a perfect crowd-pleaser that it would have no doubt been a favorite in the Reagan house, with its large gang of hungry eaters. You can use it for any special occasion, or even for a cocktail party—it's sure to become a family favorite no matter when you serve it. **Serves 4 to 6; makes 20 to 24 meatballs***

MEATBALLS

    1 pound ground beef
    1/4 pound ground pork
    3 slices white bread, crusts removed, pulsed in a food processor into bread crumbs
    1/2 cup sour cream
    1 large egg, beaten
    2 tablespoons minced yellow onion
    1/8 teaspoon ground allspice
    1/4 teaspoon freshly ground black pepper
    1 1/4 teaspoons kosher salt
    3 tablespoons unsalted butter

GRAVY

    2 cups beef stock
    2 tablespoons all-purpose flour
    Dash of ground allspice
    1/2 teaspoon onion powder
    1/2 cup sour cream

1. Make the meatballs: In a large bowl, combine all the meatball ingredients except for the butter. Working with clean hands, mix the ingredients just until incorporated. Do not overwork the mixture.

2. Using a melon baller or rounded spoon, scoop out individual meatballs. Form into spheres the size of Ping-Pong balls.

3. In a very large saucepan (or divided between two medium saucepans), melt the butter over medium heat. Brown the meatballs, turning regularly to prevent burning and to ensure even cooking. Transfer the browned meatballs to a plate and set aside.

4. Make the gravy: Add the beef stock to the saucepan in which you cooked the meatballs and stir with a wooden spoon, loosening any browned bits stuck to the pan.

5. Add the flour, allspice, and onion powder and whisk constantly until smooth. Add the sour cream, 1 teaspoon at a time, and whisk to incorporate before adding more. Continue whisking until there are no clumps.

6. Return the meatballs to the pan and simmer for 15 to 20 minutes, or until the gravy thickens. Serve hot by themselves, or with rice, noodles, or sliced baguette, as you prefer.

PIGS IN A BLANKET

Simple, delicious, and fun—what's not to love about this party-platter standard? This is a great make-ahead snack for a get-together; just prep the wieners rolled up in the dough, put them on a baking sheet, and refrigerate until you're ready to feed those hungry guests. As perfect as it is for a party or any special occasion, it's just as ideal for movie night or any family event with kids. The little ones just love the manageable size of this snack, and the combination of puffy, light dough and a super mini hot dog. It satisfies the young sense of fun and hunger alike. ***Serves 4 to 6***

One 8-ounce can crescent dinner rolls
24 cocktail wieners

1. Preheat the oven to 375°F. Grease a baking sheet.
2. Unroll the crescent dinner roll dough. Separate the dough into 8 triangles. Cut each triangle into 3 smaller triangles.
3. Lay 1 wiener along the base of a dough triangle. Roll it up, pressing to ensure the dough sticks to itself. Repeat with the rest of the cocktail wieners, and arrange the rolls on the prepared baking sheet.
4. Bake for 7 to 8 minutes, or until deep golden brown. Remove and serve warm with a ramekin of ketchup, sweet-and-sour sauce, or mustard. Or all three!

RUMAKI

Here's a blast from the past, a rich and savory favorite from cocktail parties in the 1960s. Although it will never be mistaken for a healthy canapé, rumaki are the perfect pass-around hors d'oeuvre. They will disappear as quickly as you put them out. The flavors are dominated by an appealing saltiness and the over-the-top richness of bacon and chicken liver. These party favors are enchantingly bite-size and come complete with their own toothpick handle that makes cocktail party snacking a breeze. Of course, they're just as at home on a dinner party table or buffet. ***Serves 4 to 6***

½ cup low-sodium soy sauce
2 tablespoons light brown sugar
2 teaspoons peeled and minced fresh ginger
6 chicken livers, quartered
One 8-ounce can whole water chestnuts, drained, each chestnut sliced in half
8 to 12 strips bacon

1. In a medium bowl, whisk together the soy sauce, brown sugar, and ginger. Add the chicken livers and water chestnuts, cover, and refrigerate for at least 1 hour or up to 3 hours.
2. Preheat the oven to 400°F. Line a baking sheet with aluminum foil.
3. Remove the chestnuts and chicken livers from the marinade, and transfer the marinade to a small saucepan. Bring to a boil over medium-high heat and then turn off the heat.
4. On a clean cutting board, cut the bacon strips crosswise in half. Lay out a half strip of bacon, set a chicken liver quarter in the center, and top with a water chestnut half. Wrap the two ends of the bacon strip up over the water chestnut and secure with a toothpick stuck all the way through, down into the chicken liver.
5. Arrange the rumaki on the prepared baking sheet, spacing them evenly, and brush each with a small amount of the marinade.
6. Bake for 30 to 40 minutes, or until the bacon is deep golden brown, basting periodically with the marinade. Remove from the oven and let cool for 3 minutes before serving.

BRUSCHETTA WITH TOMATOES AND BASIL

This classic Italian starter is one of the most adaptable appetizers you'll find. It makes for a simple, light beginning to a multicourse meal, but it's also wonderful as an addition to a casual lineup of tapas. It even works nicely on its own as an hors d'oeuvre. Truth is, there's really no bad way or time to serve this satisfying two-bite treat—it's even great with brunch. The recipe is adaptable in other ways as well. The garlic-rubbed bread base can serve as the foundation for toppings from prosciutto and roasted figs to olive tapenade and shaved Parmesan. Let your imagination—and your hunger—be your guide.

Serves 4 to 6

1 tablespoon extra-virgin olive oil, plus more for brushing
1 teaspoon balsamic vinegar
5 plum tomatoes, seeded and finely diced
½ teaspoon finely minced shallot
⅓ cup chopped fresh basil
1 teaspoon kosher salt
Freshly ground black pepper
1 baguette
1 large garlic clove, smashed and peeled

1. In a large bowl, combine the oil, vinegar, tomatoes, shallot, basil, salt, and pepper to taste and stir until well mixed. Refrigerate, covered, for 20 minutes or up to 1 hour.
2. Preheat the oven to 425°F.
3. Cut the baguette on the diagonal into slices ½ to ¾ inch thick. Arrange them on a baking sheet. Toast in the oven for 5 to 7 minutes, or until lightly browned on top.
4. Rub the top of each slice with the garlic, then brush with olive oil.
5. Spoon the chilled tomato mixture on top of each slice. Serve immediately.

ARTICHOKE-AND-PARMESAN DIP

*The union of artichoke and Parmesan is a marriage made in food heaven. This is a deceptively simple recipe with the most basic of flavors. Though it may not be showy or pretentious, it is incredibly delicious. The mild savory nature of the artichoke just barely cuts the richness of the cheese and mayonnaise that comprise a delightfully creamy body. Put all the parts together and you have a spectacular dip for game day or movie night. It is equal parts filling, fun, and decadent. **Serves 4***

One 14-ounce can artichoke hearts, drained and chopped
1 cup real mayonnaise
1 cup grated Parmesan cheese
1 small garlic clove, minced
Pinch of smoked paprika
Toast points, crackers, or cut vegetables, for serving

1. Preheat the oven to 375°F.
2. In a food processor, combine all the ingredients except the toast. Pulse until the texture is nearly smooth but with some chunks of artichoke remaining.
3. Transfer to a small ovenproof casserole dish and bake for 15 to 20 minutes, or until the cheese is bubbling.
4. Remove from the oven and let cool for 5 to 10 minutes. Serve warm with toast points, your favorite crackers, or crudités.

CRAB CAKES

The trick to great crab cakes is to use just enough filler ingredients to hold the cake together, but not so much that they in any way diminish or overwhelm that wonderful crab flavor. This version maintains the balance perfectly to create two-bite cakes that are appropriately delicate, sweetly rich, and moist. Serve them as party snacks and watch them fly off the plate, or add them to your next cookout menu. You can even make larger versions as a main course for a light summer meal—they're great at satisfying a big hunger without making you feel too full. **Serves 4**

SAUCE

1 cup real mayonnaise

$1/2$ small yellow onion, minced

$1/2$ dill pickle, minced

1 hard-boiled egg, peeled and minced

1 tablespoon chopped fresh chives

$1/4$ teaspoon ground mustard

Finely grated zest and juice of 1 lemon

1 tablespoon capers, drained

CRAB CAKES

1 large egg, beaten

$1/4$ cup real mayonnaise

2 tablespoons half-and-half

$1/2$ teaspoon kosher salt

Freshly ground black pepper

1 teaspoon ground mustard

1 teaspoon Worcestershire sauce

Dash of Tabasco sauce

$1/2$ teaspoon fresh lemon juice

1 teaspoon finely diced red onion

1 pound jumbo lump crabmeat

$3/4$ cup seasoned bread crumbs

3 tablespoons canola oil

1. Make the sauce: In a medium bowl, combine all the ingredients for the sauce and stir until incorporated. Cover and refrigerate until ready to use.
2. Make the crab cakes: In a large bowl, combine the egg, mayonnaise, and half-and-half. Whisk until completely incorporated. Add the salt, pepper to taste, ground mustard, Worcestershire sauce, Tabasco sauce, lemon juice, and red onion. Whisk until completely mixed.
3. Pick through the crabmeat and discard any bits of shells or hard membrane. Using a fork, stir the crabmeat into the mixture in the bowl until all the crabmeat is well coated. Add the bread crumbs and mix until they are evenly distributed throughout the mixture.
4. Using clean hands, form the crab mixture into small balls, and then flatten the balls into patties roughly 2 inches in diameter. Place the patties on a clean plate. Line a baking sheet with paper towels.
5. In a large skillet over medium-high heat, heat the oil. Fry the crab cakes, in batches, until they are dark golden brown on both sides, about 2 minutes on each side. Transfer to the lined baking sheet.
6. Let the crab cakes cool for 5 minutes, then serve with a ramekin of the sauce.

ON THE SET . . . **WITH BRIDGET**

It is always tricky filming an argument on a TV show, especially during a meal scene. As an actor, you have to do two things at once—engage in realistic emotion complete with gestures, and make sure the food props aren't in the way. Sometimes things go a little wacky. Recently, we were filming a dinner scene in which Amy Carlson and Donnie Wahlberg, as Linda and Danny Reagan, were having a bit of a blowout. Every time Amy tried to angrily respond to Donnie, her macaroni and cheese would go flying off her fork. It was hard to keep a straight face sitting across the table. It was like a food fight on the set—not the kind of battle the writers had intended.

SHRIMP COCKTAIL

*Shrimp cocktail is a perennial favorite because of the indulgent, luxuriously sweet flavor of the shellfish. It's much fancier and purely delicious than the effort it takes to make it would indicate. There are really just two keys to making absolutely fantastic shrimp cocktail: the subtle flavors you add to the cooking broth, and watching the shrimp closely so that you don't overcook it (few kitchen mistakes are quite as disappointing as rubbery shrimp). To add a bit of zest to the shrimp, we've included the tang of dry white wine—Sauvignon Blanc, but use your favorite—and a little zip courtesy of peppercorns. Pull the shrimp out of the broth as soon as they curl and turn light pink. **Serves 4***

SHRIMP

- 6 cups cold water
- 2 cups dry white wine
- 1 shallot, minced
- 1 teaspoon tricolor peppercorns
- 1 bay leaf
- 1 pound large shrimp, unpeeled

SAUCE

- 3/4 cup ketchup
- Finely grated zest and juice of 1/2 lemon
- 1 teaspoon prepared horseradish
- 1/2 teaspoon Worcestershire sauce
- Dash of Tabasco sauce

1 lemon, cut into wedges

1. Make the shrimp: In a large pot over high heat, combine the cold water, wine, shallot, peppercorns, and bay leaf and bring to a boil. Reduce to a simmer and cook for 15 minutes.
2. Add the shrimp and remove the pot from the heat. Cook, stirring occasionally, until the shrimp are light pink and curled, about 3 minutes. Drain and let the shrimp cool to room temperature.

3. Peel the shrimp, leaving the tails attached, and cut along the back edge of each to expose the vein. Remove the vein and rinse out the cut. Refrigerate the shrimp in a covered container.

4. Make the sauce: In a small bowl, combine all the ingredients for the cocktail sauce and stir until completely incorporated. Arrange the chilled shrimp on a platter around a large ramekin of the sauce, with the lemon wedges arranged around the platter.

BACON-ALMOND BUTTER TOASTS

File this one under "super-easy, super-satisfying snacks." Bacon and almond butter go together as perfectly as peanut butter and chocolate, and need only the crunchy stage of toasted bread to really shine and delight the tongue. You can substitute your favorite bread, and adjust the amount of almond butter or bacon to suit your taste. The recipe is very forgiving of changes, and the basic flavors at the heart of the snack remain intact no matter what. **Serves 4**

3 slices bagged sourdough bread
$1/4$ cup almond butter
4 strips bacon, cooked until crispy and coarsely chopped (see tip)

1. Preheat the oven to 375°F.
2. Using the mouth of a glass or a round cookie cutter, cut the bread into 2-inch rounds (about 8 rounds) and arrange them on a baking sheet. Toast the bread in the oven for about 8 minutes per side, or until golden brown on the top and bottom.
3. Spread about 1 teaspoon of the almond butter on one side of each round, mounding it in the center. Sprinkle each with some of the bacon and serve.

BLUE **BLOODS** KITCHEN **TIP**

Making bacon can be a very messy chore, but it doesn't have to be. Line a baking sheet with parchment paper and then lay the bacon strips on the paper. Cover with another sheet of parchment paper and bake in a 350°F oven until the bacon is done to your desired level of crispiness, about 12 minutes for extra crispy. The method involves no splatter and, no turning, and the parchment paper absorbs most of the grease, making cleanup a breeze.

STUFFED MUSHROOMS

Don't be surprised when the mushroom haters in your house eagerly go after this appetizer. The mushrooms themselves serve more as vessels for the myriad other flavors, and they bake to an alluring texture with just the slightest resistance between the teeth. The sweet Italian sausage is the heart of the filling, but two types of cheese and a healthy dose of bread crumbs gives the filling its creamy-crunchy sturdy body. Be careful with this one, because it's filling. You can make each mushroom more or less bite size by using smaller mushrooms. **Serves 4**

12 white or brown button mushrooms
5 tablespoons extra-virgin olive oil
$\frac{1}{4}$ cup good-quality red wine
Kosher salt and freshly ground black pepper
$\frac{1}{3}$ pound loose sweet Italian sausage
1 shallot, minced
2 garlic cloves, minced
$\frac{1}{3}$ cup panko bread crumbs
2 ounces mascarpone cheese
$\frac{1}{3}$ cup grated Pecorino Romano cheese
1 tablespoon chopped fresh flat-leaf parsley

1. Preheat the oven to 325°F.
2. Clean the mushrooms. Remove the stems, trim the ends, and finely chop the stems.
3. In a large bowl, combine 3 tablespoons of the olive oil with the red wine and season lightly with salt and pepper. Add the mushroom caps and toss until well coated. Set aside.
4. In a large pan over medium–high heat, heat the remaining 2 tablespoons olive oil. Add the sausage and break it up with a spatula as it cooks. Cook for about 5 minutes, or until completely browned and cooked through.
5. Add the shallot, garlic, and chopped mushroom stems and cook for about 3 minutes, until the chopped stems soften. Add the panko and stir until all the ingredients are evenly mixed.

6. Remove the pan from the heat, add the mascarpone, and stir until it has entirely melted. Add the Pecorino Romano and parsley and stir to combine.
7. Arrange the mushroom caps, rounded-side down, on a rimmed baking sheet. Using a spoon, scoop the sausage mixture into the caps, rounding and firming each mound.
8. Bake the stuffed mushrooms for 50 to 60 minutes, or until the mushrooms are deep brown and the stuffing is browned and crisp. Cool for about 3 minutes and serve.

MAIN COURSES

CHICKEN AND DUMPLINGS

Every once in a while you need an old-fashioned favorite just like Grandma used to make. If Grandma Reagan were around, this is the dish she would cook to cure whatever ailed you. In the process, it would make you glad to be hungry. We use the meat from dense chicken thighs, which naturally have more oils and flavor than chicken breasts, and give the final broth some very sturdy flavor. But the star is really the blander dumplings, which puff up like doughy miniature clouds and eat like fun made into food. Make this dish just once, and you'll pass it down for generations. **Serves 6**

CHICKEN

3 tablespoons olive oil

2 pounds boneless, skinless chicken thighs

Kosher salt and freshly ground black pepper

1 yellow onion, chopped

2 garlic cloves, minced

3 celery stalks, chopped

3 carrots, peeled and chopped

1 teaspoon dried thyme

$1/4$ teaspoon ground turmeric

8 cups low-sodium chicken stock

$1/2$ cup all-purpose flour

DUMPLINGS

2 cups all-purpose flour

2 teaspoons baking powder

$1/2$ teaspoon baking soda

$1/2$ teaspoon salt

Freshly ground black pepper

4 tablespoons ($1/2$ stick) unsalted butter, melted

$3/4$ cup buttermilk

1 tablespoon chopped fresh flat-leaf parsley

1. Make the chicken: In a 6-quart Dutch oven or pot, heat the olive oil over medium-high heat. Lightly season the chicken all over with salt and pepper. Brown the chicken, in batches as necessary, about 5 minutes per side. Transfer to a clean plate.

2. Add the onion and garlic to the pot and cook until the onion begins to soften, about 3 minutes. Add the celery and carrots and cook just until the carrots begin to soften, about 5 minutes.

3. Stir in the thyme and turmeric. Return the chicken to the pot and add the chicken stock. Simmer for 20 minutes, or until the chicken is completely cooked through.

4. Remove the chicken, shred the meat with two forks (or pull it apart), and return it to the pot.

5. In a medium bowl, whisk together the flour with 2 cups of the cooking liquid and season liberally with salt and pepper. Slowly whisk the mixture back into the pot and simmer until thickened, about 7 minutes.

6. While the broth is simmering, make the dumplings: In a large bowl, combine the flour, baking powder, baking soda, salt, and pepper to taste and whisk until completely mixed. Whisk in the melted butter and buttermilk.

7. Reduce the heat under the broth to medium-low and drop the batter into the broth in large spoonfuls. Simmer, covered, until the dumplings are firm, about 15 minutes. Serve the stew with 1 dumpling per bowl, sprinkled with the parsley.

BAKED SHELLS

Some dishes are pure and simple comfort food, and this cheesy delight wears the description proudly. The shells almost act as individual servings, overflowing with a triple-cheese mixture as luscious as any lasagna. We use a meat sauce for the big way it cuts the richness of the cheese, but you can opt for a marinara if you like that better. Either way, this is the ideal make-ahead-and-freeze weeknight meal for a big family or crowd. Whether you make it beforehand or not, you can save time and energy by substituting jarred sauce for the homemade version we use. ***Serves 6 to 8***

One 12-ounce box jumbo shells
Two 15-ounce tubs whole-milk ricotta cheese
2 large eggs
1 pound mozzarella cheese, shredded
1/3 cup grated Parmesan cheese, plus more for sprinkling
Kosher salt and freshly ground black pepper
3 cups Meat Sauce (page 245)

1. Preheat the oven to 350°F.
2. Fill a large pot with cold water (at least 4 quarts). Heavily salt the water and bring to a boil over high heat.
3. Cook the shells in the water for about 8 minutes, or until just cooked. Drain and rinse with cold water.
4. While the shells are cooking, combine the ricotta and eggs in a large bowl. Stir until completely mixed. Stir in the mozzarella. Add the Parmesan and mix in thoroughly. Liberally season the mixture with salt and pepper.
5. Using a teaspoon, fill the cooled shells with the cheese mixture.
6. Spread about 1 cup of the meat sauce over the bottom of a glass casserole dish. Line the dish with the stuffed shells. Cover with the remaining meat sauce and sprinkle Parmesan over the top. (You can freeze the shells at this point, for later use.)
7. Bake the shells for 1 hour. Serve hot.

CHICKEN POT PIE

Sure, you could warm up store-bought pot pies in a jiffy, but they wouldn't hold a candle to this time-tested kitchen gem. Our pot pie is served family style, but if you prefer individual servings, divide the filling among miniature casserole dishes; you'll need more pie crust, but the process will be the same. In any case, the filling is meant to be captured in a hearty, thick sauce. We've used chicken breasts, but chopped or shredded grilled chicken thigh or rotisserie chicken meat would add a bit of flavor and even a little smokiness to the filling. **Serves 4 to 6**

2 frozen pie crust sheets, defrosted
4 tablespoons (½ stick) unsalted butter
½ cup finely chopped yellow onion
1 cup finely chopped carrots
¼ cup all-purpose flour
½ teaspoon salt

½ teaspoon black pepper
1 teaspoon lemon juice
2 cups chicken stock
½ cup half-and-half
2 cups chopped cooked chicken breast meat
1 cup frozen peas

1. Preheat the oven to 425°F. Line a 9-inch glass pie plate with one of the pie crust sheets.
2. In a large pot over medium heat, melt the butter. Add the onion and cook until softened. Add the carrots and cook for 5 minutes.
3. Slowly add the flour, stirring, to coat. Season with the salt and pepper, then add the lemon juice and stock. Cook, stirring, until the sauce is smooth. Stir in the half-and-half and cook until thickened and heated through.
4. Remove the pot from the heat and stir in the chicken and peas. Spoon the filling into the lined pie plate. Cover the top with the second pie crust sheet and pinch the edges of the bottom and top crusts together. Trim off any extra dough. Cut three slits in the top to allow steam to escape during baking.
5. Bake for 30 minutes, or until the top is a deep golden brown Remove from the oven and let rest for 5 minutes before slicing and serving.

BAKED FISH AND CHIPS

*Fish and chips is the United Kingdom's original fast food, although it's a fast food chock-full of omega-3 fatty acids and fiber. Still-hot strips of fried fish wrapped in newspaper with sizzling, heavily salted French fries (or "chips" on that side of the pond) sprinkled with malt vinegar is the perfect on-the-go meal—especially when you're stuck in damp, cold weather. Our baked version does justice to this classic, retaining the filling goodness of the original, but with a whole lot less grease and free radicals. We replaced the traditional fries with true American potato chips, but you can bake up fries instead—just follow the directions in the box on page 92. **Serves 4***

3 Russet potatoes
¼ cup canola oil
¼ teaspoon cayenne pepper
Sea salt
½ cup all-purpose flour
Kosher salt and freshly ground black pepper
2 large eggs, lightly beaten
2 cups finely crushed cornflakes
1½ pounds skinless cod fillets, (or substitute any firm white-fleshed fish) cut
   into 2-inch-long pieces
Tartar sauce and malt vinegar, for serving

1. Preheat the oven to 425°F. Position the racks at the top third and bottom third of the oven. Coat two rimmed baking sheets with cooking spray.
2. Scrub the potatoes and slice crosswise into ¼-inch-thick chips. In a large bowl, whisk together the oil and cayenne. Add the potatoes and toss until evenly coated. Sprinkle liberally with sea salt and toss again.
3. Spread out the chips on one prepared baking sheet in an even layer. Place the sheet on the top oven rack and bake until deep golden brown and crispy, about 25 minutes.
4. While the chips are baking, place the flour in a wide, shallow bowl, season with

kosher salt and black pepper, and whisk until well combined. Pour the eggs into a second wide, shallow bowl, and put the cornflakes in a third bowl.

5. Working with one piece at a time, dip the fish in the flour and shake off any excess. Dunk it in the egg, ensuring it is well coated on all sides. Let any excess drip off. Press the fish into the cornflakes and gently shake off any excess.

6. Place the fish on the second prepared baking sheet. Put the sheet in the oven on the bottom rack, when the chips have about 10 minutes left to cook. Cook the fish for 12 to 15 minutes, or until the cornflake crust is browned and crispy.

7. Remove the chips, toss with more sea salt as needed, and set aside until cool enough to handle. Remove the fish and divide among four plates (or paper-lined baskets). Divide the chips among the plates. Serve hot with tartar sauce and/or malt vinegar.

BLUE **BLOODS** KITCHEN **TIPS**

Whether you want to substitute fries for the chips in our Baked Fish and Chips recipe or just want a helping of fries for any reason, bake them as a healthier alternative to frying. Cut two large Russet potatoes lengthwise into thick matchsticks. Pat them dry, and then toss them in a bowl with a drizzle of canola oil until they're evenly coated. Bake in a preheated 425°F oven on a baking sheet that has been sprayed with cooking spray, for 15 to 20 minutes. Turn the fries halfway through. When they are well browned, remove the fries and toss with a sprinkle of sea salt. Serve when cool enough to handle.

BAKED ZITI

If you grew up with the kind of Italian neighborhood friends that the fictional Frank Reagan did, you'd know that the smell of baked ziti coming out of the oven, topped with bubbling hot cheese and steaming meat sauce, is a little bit of heaven on Earth. We didn't stray far from the classic with ours, with a combination of hot and sweet Italian sausages. That means there's a little spicy edge to this version. If your crowd is shy about spiciness, you can dial back the heat by changing the ratio to use more sweet sausage (or use just sweet sausage, as you prefer). For a little extra richness, use diced San Marzano tomatoes. They can be harder to find and always a bit more expensive, but the added flavor is well worth it. **Serves 6**

One 16-ounce box ziti
2 tablespoons olive oil
1 yellow onion, diced
2 garlic cloves, minced
$\frac{3}{4}$ pound loose hot Italian sausage (or use links, with meat removed from casings)
$\frac{3}{4}$ pound loose sweet Italian sausage (or use links, with meat removed
   from casings)
1 tablespoon tomato paste
$\frac{1}{4}$ teaspoon kosher salt
$\frac{1}{4}$ teaspoon freshly ground black pepper
One 28-ounce can petite-diced tomatoes
$\frac{1}{4}$ cup chopped fresh basil
2 cups shredded fresh mozzarella cheese
1 cup grated Parmesan cheese

1. Preheat the oven to 375°F. Coat a 4-quart casserole dish or roasting pan with cooking spray.
2. Fill a large pot with at least 4 quarts of water, salt it heavily so that it tastes like the sea, and bring to a boil. Add the ziti and cook until al dente, about 8 minutes. (Err on the side of caution. If the pasta is a little undercooked, it's okay; it will finish cooking in the oven.)

3. While the pasta cooks, heat the olive oil in a large skillet over medium-high heat. Add the onion and garlic and cook until the onion begins to soften.

4. Add the sausage and lower the heat to medium. Cook, using a wooden spoon to break up the sausage, until it is completely browned. Drain off any excess grease.

5. Add the tomato paste, salt, pepper, and tomatoes and bring to a boil. Cover, reduce the heat to a simmer for 10 minutes, stirring occasionally.

6. Return the drained pasta to the pot and add the sausage mixture. Add the basil and stir well to thoroughly mix it in.

7. Layer half the ziti mixture in the prepared casserole dish. Top with half the mozzarella and Parmesan cheeses. Layer the rest of the ziti mixture on top, and cover with the remaining cheese.

8. Cover the dish with aluminum foil and bake the casserole for 15 minutes. Remove the foil and bake for 15 minutes more, or until the top is browned and starting to crisp. Serve hot.

TWO-ALARM CHILI

*Putting your own stamp on chili is all about understanding where your family's taste-bud thermostat is set. Our version has just a bit of fire (which is why it's two, rather than three, alarms), but combines amazing flavors and textures including three different types of beans. You can turn up the heat when you make this chili by adding chopped jalapeños, or—if you're truly adventurous—much hotter varieties such as Scotch Bonnet peppers. Use about a teaspoon of minced hot peppers and add them in with the spices. Fine-tune the fiery nature of your chili by increasing or decreasing the amount of crushed red pepper flakes. And although we use lean turkey to keep our chili low-fat, you can use beef, pork sausage, or a combination, to suit your own tastes. Get it right, and you'll have an empty pot by the end of dinner. **Serves 6***

1 pound extra-lean ground turkey (or substitute lean ground beef sirloin or lean sweet pork sausage)

2 tablespoons canola oil

1 yellow onion, chopped

3 garlic cloves, chopped

2 celery stalks, chopped

5 carrots, peeled and chopped

2 tablespoons chili powder

1 teaspoon ground cumin

1 teaspoon crushed red pepper flakes

$\frac{1}{2}$ teaspoon smoked paprika

1 tablespoon dried parsley

1 teaspoon kosher salt

1 teaspoon freshly ground black pepper

$\frac{1}{2}$ cup beer

One 28-ounce can diced tomatoes

One 15-ounce can black beans, drained but not rinsed

One 15-ounce can kidney beans, drained but not rinsed

One 15-ounce can pinto beans, drained but not rinsed

$\frac{1}{2}$ cup water

1. In a large saucepan or skillet over medium-high heat, brown the ground turkey. Drain off any excess grease.
2. While the turkey is browning, heat the canola oil in a large pot over medium-high heat. Add the onion, garlic, and celery and cook until the onion begins to soften, about 3 minutes.
3. Stir in the carrots and cook for about 5 minutes. Add the browned turkey meat, chili powder, cumin, red pepper flakes, paprika, parsley, salt, and black pepper and stir until the ingredients are evenly coated with the spices. Cook for 3 minutes, then add the beer, scraping up any browned bits from the bottom of the pot.
4. Add the tomatoes and beans, and stir to combine all the ingredients thoroughly. Add the water and reduce the heat as necessary to maintain a simmer. Simmer for 1 hour, or until the sauce has thickened and the carrots are tender.
5. Serve hot with a sprinkling of cheddar cheese or a dollop of sour cream, as you desire.

CORNED BEEF **AND** CABBAGE **WITH** GUINNESS

If ever a TV family knew how to celebrate St. Patrick's Day, it's the Reagans. And what would any St. Paddy's day celebration be without traditional corned beef and cabbage? This version comes courtesy of Len Cariou, who plays patriarch Henry Reagan on the show. In this Emerald Isle classic, a tough, inexpensive cut of meat (beef brisket, in this case) is cooked a long time in ample juices, so that it breaks down and becomes fall-apart tender. Throw in some sturdy vegetables and an "Irish truffle" or two (better known as potatoes), and you have one of the most satisfying meals you'll ever taste—even if the beer isn't dyed green. This is a filling dish that feeds a large crowd—so invite the whole family! **Serves 6 to 8**

One 3½- to 4-pound flat-cut corned beef brisket
One 12- to 14-ounce bottle or can Guinness draught (not stout)
1 large yellow onion, cut into wedges
4 garlic cloves, peeled and smashed
½ teaspoon tricolor peppercorns
3 large sprigs fresh thyme
2 bay leaves
¼ teaspoon ground allspice
5 yellow potatoes, scrubbed and halved
1 pound carrots, peeled and chopped into 2-inch pieces
1 large head green cabbage, sliced into wedges

1. Rinse the corned beef with cold water and pat dry. In a Dutch oven over medium-high heat, combine the corned beef, beer, and enough water to cover the meat by 2 inches. Add the onion and garlic.
2. Wrap the peppercorns, thyme sprigs, and bay leaves in a piece of cheesecloth to make a pouch, and tie closed with a bit of kitchen twine. Add the pouch to the Dutch oven. Add the allspice.
3. Bring the liquid to a boil, then reduce to maintain a gentle simmer. Cover and simmer for 3 hours, adding more water as necessary to keep the meat covered.

4. Add the potatoes, carrots, and cabbage and simmer for 45 minutes, or until the carrots are fork-tender (you can wait for 20 minutes before adding the cabbage if you prefer it to have a sturdier texture).

5. Transfer the meat to a cutting board and slice it against the grain. Arrange on a serving platter with the vegetables around it (remove and discard the cheesecloth pouch). Dress with a bit of the cooking juices and serve.

HERB-ROASTED **CHICKEN**

*Many home cooks have not yet discovered just how great cooking a whole chicken can be. If you're one of those poor souls, it's time you learned. Perhaps the most wonderful thing about a whole chicken is that it is a blank slate for your favorite flavors, from savory to sweet. The thoughtful combination of herbs in this dish gives the chicken a piquant, slightly Mediterranean flair, but you can adjust the herb blend to reflect your own preferences. No matter what, you'll wind up with more delicious meat than you might think, and the bones can serve as the perfect base for a delectable chicken soup or useful chicken stock. **Serves 4 to 6***

One 4-pound whole chicken
3 tablespoons extra-virgin olive oil
1 tablespoon chopped fresh rosemary leaves
1 tablespoon chopped fresh thyme leaves
1 teaspoon dried oregano
1 teaspoon kosher salt
$1/2$ teaspoon freshly ground black pepper
2 sprigs fresh rosemary
2 sprigs fresh thyme
$1/2$ yellow onion, quartered
$1/2$ lemon, quartered

1. Preheat the oven to 425°F.
2. Remove and discard the giblets. Rinse the chicken in cold water, including flushing out the cavity. Pat dry and allow the chicken to come to room temperature.
3. In a small bowl, combine the oil, chopped rosemary, chopped thyme, oregano, salt, and pepper. Using your hands, rub the mixture all over the chicken and into the cavity. Make sure the chicken is entirely coated.
4. Place the rosemary and thyme sprigs, and onion and lemon quarters inside the chicken. Tie the legs together with kitchen twine (this is done for appearance). You can skip this if it doesn't matter to you.

5. Place the chicken, breast-side up, in a roasting pan. Roast for 1½ hours, rotating the pan and basting the chicken with the pan juices every 15 to 20 minutes, until the skin is deep golden brown and crispy, and an instant-read thermometer inserted into the thickest part of the thigh registers 165°F.

6. Transfer the chicken to a serving platter and let it rest for 10 minutes before carving. Serve with Roasted Potatoes (page 173), Roasted Root Vegetables (page 195), or your favorite sides.

STANDING RIB ROAST WITH CIPOLLINI ONION SAUCE

Both the fictional Frank Reagan and the man who plays him, Tom Selleck, are down-to-earth, no-apologies meat eaters. You can't get much meatier than a standing rib roast, especially one treated with simple seasonings and allowed to cook to luscious tenderness. We serve ours with a to-die-for cipollini onion sauce that would go just as well over chicken breasts or even on sturdy pasta. The secret lies in the red wine base that accents and brings out the sweet flavors of the roasted onions. Serve the sauce on the side for those meat eaters who don't want to dilute the pure pleasure of an excellent cut of meat perfectly cooked. **Serves 6 to 8**

SAUCE

1/4 cup plus 2 tablespoons extra-virgin olive oil

2 teaspoons balsamic vinegar

2 pounds cipollini onions, trimmed and peeled

1 tablespoon unsalted butter

3 garlic cloves, minced

Kosher salt and freshly ground black pepper

3 cups high-quality dry red wine

RIB ROAST

1/2 cup kosher salt

1/4 cup freshly ground black pepper

1/4 cup garlic salt

One 6- to 8-pound standing rib roast

1. Preheat the oven to 425°F.
2. Roast the onions for the sauce: In a large bowl, combine 1/4 cup of the olive oil with the vinegar. Add the onions and toss until they are completely coated. Transfer the onions to a rimmed baking sheet and drizzle with any remaining dressing.

3. Roast the onions for 50 to 60 minutes until well browned and completely soft. Transfer to a cutting board.

4. Increase the oven temperature to 450°F.

5. Make the rib roast: In a small bowl, combine the kosher salt, pepper, and garlic salt for the roast and stir until thoroughly mixed. Coat the roast with the rub all around. Put the roast in a roasting pan equipped with a rack and roast for 20 minutes.

6. Lower the oven temperature to 350°F, and roast for about 18 minutes per pound, or until the internal temperature registers 125°F for medium-rare (130° to 135°F for medium). Remove from the oven and let rest for 15 to 20 minutes before slicing.

7. When the roast has about 30 minutes of cooking time left, start the sauce: Using a sharp knife, finely dice the roasted onions.

8. In a large skillet over medium-high heat, combine the remaining 2 tablespoons olive oil and the butter. When the butter has melted, add the garlic and cook for 3 minutes. Season with kosher salt and pepper.

9. Add the wine and onions, reduce to maintain a gentle simmer, and cook for about 40 minutes, or until the liquid reduces and thickens to the consistency of syrup. Serve the roast, sliced, with the sauce on the side.

ON THE SET . . . **WITH BRIDGET**

Sami Gayle, who plays my daughter, Nicky, on *Blue Bloods*, was a late addition to the cast. The crew didn't have a lot of time to prepare for the fact that she's a devout vegetarian. In her first family dinner scene, she was seated across from me. We were served meatballs and for each take, she would take a bite of meatball and then spit it into a napkin at the end of the take. To make things worse, one of the young boys (the guilty party will remain nameless) who play her cousins on the show sneezed right over the plate of meatballs. We all sat there, shocked, for a few seconds, and then I looked at Sami and said, "I guess you really won't be eating them now." That became a running joke between us: "Don't eat the meatballs!"

ROASTED PORK LOIN

Experience the incredibly luxurious flavors of this succulent meat and you'll be surprised at just how healthy it is. Although—with the help of the herb-and-garlic rub—the meat stays decadently moist throughout the cooking process, it is an exceptionally lean and healthy chicken alternative. The simple sauce we include with our recipe is high on flavor, but doesn't add too many calories. You'll find that even the younger members of the family are drawn to the clean, elegant flavors and uncomplicated nature of pork loin. Save any extra for sandwiches and you'll be happy you did. **Serves 4 to 6**

3 garlic cloves, finely minced

¼ cup extra-virgin olive oil

1 bay leaf, crushed

2 tablespoons minced fresh chives

Kosher salt and freshly ground black pepper

One 1½- to 2-pound boneless pork loin

2 shallots, minced

1 cup good-quality red wine

2 tablespoons cold unsalted butter, cubed

1. In a small bowl, whisk together the garlic, olive oil, bay leaf, and chives. Liberally season with salt and pepper, then rub the loin all over with the garlic mixture and refrigerate for 2 hours or up to overnight.
2. Preheat the oven to 425°F.
3. Remove the loin from the refrigerator and let it come to room temperature. Heat a large sauté pan over medium-high heat, and then sear the loin on all sides. Transfer it to a roasting pan and roast for 20 minutes, or until an instant-read thermometer registers 145°F.
4. Remove the loin from the oven and transfer to a cutting board. Tent with aluminum foil and let it rest for about 10 minutes.
5. Heat the drippings in the roasting pan over medium-high heat. Add the shallots and cook until they begin to soften. Add the wine and bring to a boil, then

reduce the heat to maintain a simmer. Cook until the sauce has reduced by about half and thickened.

6. Remove the sauce from the heat and whisk in the cold butter, a cube at a time. Cut the pork into ½-inch slices, dress each portion with the sauce, and serve.

SANDWICH OPTIONS

Leftover pork loin makes for a truly spectacular and sophisticated sandwich. Slice the loin thinly. Then peel and core a Granny Smith apple and cut it into the thinnest slices possible (use a mandoline, if you have one). Cut a ciabatta roll in half and slather the cut faces with high-quality honey mustard. Layer the apple slices on one half, top with the pork loin, and set the other half of the bread on top.

PITCH-PERFECT PIZZA

*If you're looking for a wonderful weekend treat that provides its own fun, look no further. Children are always amazed when you make pizza at home, and many adults are also a little surprised that it can be done so easily. To do this one right, you'll need a pizza stone. Fortunately, they are widely available, inexpensive, and ensure the ultimate crust. The beauty of our recipe is that you don't need a mixer; the dough is blended without a dough hook. We divide the dough to make two large pizzas, but you can divide it further into individual-pizza size—and let every member of the family choose his or her own toppings. Flattening out the pizza is part of the fun, as is spreading the sauce, scattering the cheese, and laying down those toppings. **Serves 6; makes two 12-inch pizzas***

DOUGH

    1 teaspoon extra-virgin olive oil, plus more as needed

    One 1/4-ounce package active dry yeast

    1 1/2 teaspoons table salt

    3 cups all-purpose flour (substitute cake flour for a crunchier crust),
       plus more for dusting

SAUCE

    2 tablespoons extra-virgin olive oil

    1/2 yellow onion, finely minced

    3 garlic cloves, finely minced

    1/2 teaspoon crushed red pepper flakes

    1 teaspoon dried oregano

    1/2 teaspoon kosher salt

    Freshly ground black pepper

    2 tablespoons tomato paste

    1/4 cup red wine

    One 28-ounce can crushed tomatoes

    1 teaspoon finely chopped fresh basil, plus about 12 leaves for topping

    One 16-ounce bag shredded mozzarella cheese

    Toppings of your choice

1. Oil a 2-quart glass bowl. Dust a large, clean work surface with flour.
2. Make the dough: In a large bowl, combine the yeast with the 1 cup of warm water, as close to 110°F as possible. Add the salt and olive oil, and let proof for 5 minutes.
3. Sift in half the flour and mix until completely incorporated. Sift in the rest of the flour and use your hands to mix the dough until it is a uniform texture. Transfer to the floured work surface.
4. Knead the dough for 5 minutes, or until it is elastic and smooth. Dust with flour as you work, until the dough is no longer sticky. Transfer the dough to the prepared glass bowl and cover with a damp dish towel. Place the bowl in a warm spot to rise until the dough has doubled in volume, 1 to 1½ hours.
5. While the dough is rising, make the sauce: In a large saucepan, over medium heat heat the oil. Add the onion and garlic and cook until the onion is soft.
6. Sprinkle in the red pepper flakes, oregano, salt, and black pepper. Stir and cook for 1 minute. Add the tomato paste, stir to distribute evenly, and cook for 2 minutes.
7. Add the wine and deglaze the pan, scraping up any bits stuck to the bottom. Cook, stirring, for 2 minutes. Add the tomatoes and the chopped basil. Reduce the heat to maintain a simmer and cook for 20 minutes, or until thickened. Remove from the heat.
8. Put a pizza stone in the oven and preheat the oven to 500°F.
9. Assemble the pizza: Remove the risen pizza dough from the bowl and cut in half. Form into two balls on a floured work surface. Press down with your fingertips all around one ball, working in toward the center, to flatten it into a circle. Carefully pull on the edges as you rotate the circle, until the dough is roughly 12 inches in diameter and an even thickness. Repeat with the second dough ball.
10. Heavily flour (or scatter corn meal over) a large cutting board or pizza peel. Place one of the pizza rounds on the board. Brush the dough with olive oil. Using a ladle or spoon, spread the sauce over the pizza round. Sprinkle a layer of mozzarella on top and add any additional toppings you prefer.
11. Transfer to the pizza stone and bake the pizza for about 12 minutes, or until the cheese is bubbling and the crust is golden brown. Remove the pizza from the oven and bake the second pizza in the same way. Slice with a pizza cutter and serve.

PIT-ZA

Not enough time to make the pizza from scratch? Try this easy, quick, and delicious substitute—courtesy of Wendy! *Serves 4*

1 white onion, thinly sliced
2 zucchini, thinly sliced
8 ounces white button mushrooms, stems trimmed, thinly sliced
1/4 cup plus 2 tablespoons extra-virgin olive oil
Salt and pepper
2 cups chopped spinach
4 pita breads or plain naan
1/2 cup tomato sauce
12 ounces shredded mozzarella
Pitted black olives (optional)
2 teaspoons dried oregano (optional)
Shredded chicken (optional)

1. Preheat the oven to 425°F.
2. In a large bowl, combine the onion, zucchini, and mushrooms with 2 tablespoons of the olive oil. Toss until the vegetables are coated and then season liberally with salt and pepper.
3. Spread the vegetables on a baking sheet and roast for 5 minutes. Transfer to a large bowl, add the spinach, and toss to combine.
4. Arrange the pitas on a baking sheet and brush them with the remaining 1/4 cup olive oil. Divide the tomato sauce among the pitas and spread evenly across the top.
5. Spread an even layer of mozzarella across the top of each pita, and then divide the roasted vegetables among the four pizzas.
6. Sprinkle with the olives, oregano, and/or chicken, if using.
7. Bake for 5 to 8 minutes, or until crispy. Let cool for about 3 minutes before cutting and serving.

JILLIE SELLECK'S SHEPHERD'S PIE

Tom Selleck's wife, Jillie, gave us this recipe—one of Tom's favorites. Jillie is British (and a talented dancer and actress in her own right), and she's well acquainted with this working-class British standard. The true original version uses lamb, but Jillie has substituted beef to Americanize it for her husband—which makes it closer to English "cottage pie." She also makes it without the traditional veggies because that's how Tom prefers it. You can make up your own mind about whether to put them in or not. In any case, the mashed potato topping serves as a delectable crust that keeps the filling from drying out.

Serves 6 to 8

TOPPING

1$\frac{1}{2}$ pounds Russet potatoes, peeled and cubed

2 tablespoons unsalted butter, melted

$\frac{3}{4}$ cup heavy cream

1 large egg yolk

$\frac{1}{2}$ teaspoon kosher salt

$\frac{1}{2}$ teaspoon freshly ground black pepper

FILLING

2 tablespoons canola oil

1 yellow onion, diced

2 garlic cloves, minced

1 large carrot, peeled and diced

1$\frac{1}{2}$ pounds ground beef (97% lean)

1 teaspoon chopped fresh rosemary leaves

$\frac{1}{2}$ teaspoon paprika

1 teaspoon kosher salt

$\frac{1}{2}$ teaspoon freshly ground black pepper

2 tablespoons all-purpose flour

1 cup beef broth

1 tablespoon Worcestershire sauce

$\frac{1}{2}$ cup frozen corn kernels (optional)

$\frac{1}{2}$ cup frozen peas (optional)

1. Make the topping: Put the potatoes in a large pot, cover them with cold water, and bring to a boil. Boil for about 10 minutes, or just until the potatoes are fork-tender. Drain and transfer to a large bowl.
2. In a small bowl, whisk together the butter, cream, and egg yolk. Season with the salt and pepper and pour the mixture over the potatoes. Using a potato masher or mixer, mash the potatoes until they are smooth and free of lumps.
3. Make the filling: In a large pot over medium-high heat, heat the oil. Add the onion, garlic, and carrot and cook until the onion begins to soften.
4. Preheat the oven to 425°F.
5. Add the meat and brown it, stirring frequently and breaking up any large clumps with a wooden spoon. When the meat is completely browned, add the rosemary, paprika, salt, and pepper and stir until all the ingredients are well mixed.
6. Add the flour and stir until it coats the meat. Pour in the broth, add the Worcestershire sauce, and bring to a boil. Reduce the heat to maintain a simmer and cook until the sauce has reduced by about one-third and thickened.
7. Add the corn and peas (if using), stir them in, and cook for 1 minute.
8. Transfer the meat filling to a 2-quart oven-safe casserole dish. Spread the potatoes in an even layer over top of the filling, starting with the edges. Make sure the edges are sealed and that there are no holes in the potato layer.
9. Bake the pie for about 20 minutes, or until the top begins to brown and the filling is bubbling. Transfer to a wire rack to rest for 5 to 10 minutes before serving.

LONDON BROIL

London broil is not a cut of meat, but a style of preparation for any thick steak. We use top round because it is naturally more tender than other common choices. But no matter which cut you choose, the two secrets to a great London broil are to cook the steak no more than medium-rare, and to slice it against the grain—both ensure that the meat is exceedingly tender. As with all London broils, ours is marinated to tenderize the meat and to add a few subtle flavor accents. Cook it right, though, and this dish is all about deep, beefy flavor—perfect for the true meat lovers in your crowd. **Serves 4 to 6**

½ cup extra-virgin olive oil
2 tablespoons Worcestershire sauce
3 large garlic cloves
2 sprigs fresh thyme
¼ cup balsamic vinegar
1 teaspoon kosher salt
1 teaspoon freshly ground black pepper
1 top round London broil (about 2 pounds)

1. In a large bowl, combine the oil, Worcestershire sauce, garlic, thyme, vinegar, salt, and pepper. Stir until thoroughly mixed.
2. Put the meat in a clean 1-gallon resealable refrigerator bag (or use a covered glass container). Pour in the marinade. Squeeze out as much air as possible and seal the bag. Turn to coat the meat. Refrigerate for 4 hours or up to overnight.
3. Preheat a grill or heat a grill pan over medium-high heat. Remove the meat from the marinade, allowing any extra to drip off. Discard any leftover marinade. Grill the meat for about 7 minutes per side, or until an instant-read thermometer registers 135°F (for medium-rare).
4. Transfer the steak to a cutting board and let the meat rest for 10 minutes before cutting into thin slices against the grain. Serve with your favorite side or a salad.

SANDWICH **OPTIONS**

Ready for an unforgettable and filling steak sandwich that will ruin you for all other steak sandwiches? Try this on for size. Make Garlic Bread as described on page 193, but cut the bread to the length of a hoagie roll, rather than slicing it. Slice the London Broil thinner than normal and shingle the meat slices on one-half. Coat the other half with a very thin layer of meat sauce from the London Broil, and dot the meat with horseradish. Lay the top half of the bread on top of the meat, and prepare to awe your taste buds. (You can also substitute the Flank Steak on page 169 for the London Broil.)

GLAZED HAM

How about a holiday centerpiece that requires little work to produce a phenomenally flavorful main course? This ham fills the bill in a big way. Juicy, with a deep rich flavor, a spiral-cut ham is already the perfect way to feed a holiday gathering. And a sweet and tangy glaze puts it over the top. You can customize this glaze to your own preferences— just be careful to keep it thick enough to coat and stick, but not so thick that it becomes a rub. Cook the glaze just until it has thickened and is tacky on the surface of the ham, and you'll have the perfect coating to accent the cured pork flavors. The best part? Scrumptious leftovers for days. **Serves 6 to 8**

One 9- to 12-pound spiral-cut, bone-in ham
$1\frac{1}{2}$ cups packed brown sugar
3 tablespoons bourbon
1 tablespoon balsamic vinegar
1 teaspoon ground mustard
Finely grated zest of 1 orange
1 tablespoon fresh orange juice

1. Preheat the oven to 275°F.
2. Place the ham in a roasting pan, flat-side down. Tent the ham with aluminum foil.
3. Bake for 12 minutes per pound. Remove the ham and increase the oven temperature to 425°F.
4. While the ham is cooking, combine the brown sugar, bourbon, vinegar, mustard, orange zest, and orange juice in a small pot over medium-low heat. Cook, whisking, until the sugar dissolves. Remove from the heat and let cool slightly.
5. Remove the ham from the oven and brush the glaze evenly all over the surface of the ham. Return it to the oven and bake, uncovered, for 20 minutes, or until the glaze is shiny and set. Let the ham rest for 10 minutes before serving.

SANDWICH OPTIONS

Don't eat your leftover holiday ham plain! Give it new life and a French accent with an interesting twist on traditional ham and cheese. This sandwich takes its inspiration from the classic French Croque Monsieur.

2 teaspoons real mayonnaise
1 teaspoon Dijon mustard
½ teaspoon freshly ground black pepper
¼ teaspoon chopped fresh tarragon
½ teaspoon chopped cornichons
1 tablespoon unsalted butter, softened
2 slices thickly cut French bread
Sliced ham
Sliced Gruyère cheese
Frisée

1. In a small bowl, whisk together the mayonnaise, mustard, pepper, tarragon, and cornichons.
2. Butter one side of each slice of bread. On the unbuttered side of one slice, layer the ham, Gruyère, and frisée, in that order.
3. Spread the unbuttered side of the second bread slice with the mayonnaise mixture and place it on top of the frisée.
4. Heat a heavy skillet over medium-high heat. Toast the sandwich on each side, until the surface of the bread is golden brown and the cheese has melted, about 2 minutes per side. Slice and serve hot.

MEAT LOAF

*Meat loaf is a lot like a mom's hug—it's easy to forget how great it is until you go a long time without one. This meat loaf is a little more special than most, thanks to a trio of meats that add flavor and—most important—maintain moisture no matter how long you cook it. We also used our own special spice blend to give the meat loaf a wonderfully subtle savory flavor that is perfectly complemented by the sweetness of the glaze. Meat loaf glazes are like icing on a cake; apply the glaze thick or thin, based on your own preferences. Refrigerate any leftovers for soul-satisfying sandwiches or unrivaled delicious quick snacks. **Serves 4***

MEAT LOAF

½ pound ground beef (80% lean)

½ pound ground pork

½ pound ground veal

¾ cup old-fashioned rolled oats

1 large egg

¼ cup minced yellow onion

1 teaspoon kosher salt

1 teaspoon celery seed

½ tablespoon dried parsley, crushed

1 teaspoon dried oregano

¼ teaspoon freshly ground black pepper

1 cup tomato juice

GLAZE

¼ cup tomato paste

¼ cup Worcestershire sauce

3 tablespoons tomato juice

Freshly ground black pepper

1. Preheat the oven to 400°F.

2. Make the meat loaf: In a large glass bowl, combine all the ingredients for the meat loaf. Wash your hands, then use your hands to mix the meat loaf until all the ingredients are evenly incorporated. Transfer the meat loaf mixture to a 9 x 5-inch loaf pan.

3. Make the glaze: Combine all the ingredients for the glaze in a small bowl and whisk until completely incorporated. Coat the top of the meat loaf with the glaze using a spoon or brush.

4. Bake the meat loaf for 45 to 60 minutes, or until the internal temperature of the loaf registers 160°F on an instant read thermometer. Remove from the oven and let the meat loaf rest for about 5 minutes. Slice and serve warm.

SANDWICH OPTIONS

A cold meat-loaf sandwich is one of life's greatest simple pleasures, right up there with spring sunshine on your face and the smell of a fresh-cut lawn. There's nothing fancy about it: Layer a thick slab of meat loaf between two slices of plain white sandwich bread, and coat the meat loaf with as much ketchup as you like. Cut the sandwich in half for easy handling and enjoy!

SAMI GAYLE'S **TURKEY** MEAT **LOAF**

Sami Gayle, the actor who plays Nicky Reagan-Boyle on Blue Bloods, *provided this alternative to the traditional version of meat loaf. This option cuts down on the fat a bit, without giving up precious protein—all with just as much flavor!* **Serves 6 to 8**

7 carrots, peeled and coarsely chopped

2 yellow onions, peeled and finely diced

4 garlic cloves, minced

2 pounds lean ground turkey

4 ounces applesauce

1 cup ketchup

½ teaspoon salt

½ teaspoon pepper

¾ cup Italian-seasoned bread crumbs

1. Preheat the oven to 400°F.
2. Shred the carrots in a food processor and transfer to a large bowl. Add the onions and garlic and stir with a fork.
3. Add the turkey, applesauce, ¾ cup of the ketchup, salt, pepper, and bread crumbs. Wash your hands, then use your hands to mix the meat loaf just until the ingredients are incorporated.
4. Divide the mixture between two 9 x 5-inch loaf pans. Top each loaf with a thin layer of the remaining ketchup.
5. Cook for 1 hour, or until both loaves are brown and the topping is tacky. Serve hot.

OSSO BUCO

*Old World Italian cooks were not fond of wasting any possible cooking ingredient. That's how they came to use veal shank—essentially a cross section of the leg bone. The meat is naturally tough, so rural cooks would stew it all day, letting the process of braising break down the meat until it was fall-apart tender. We prefer the more modern version of the dish, which includes tomatoes. The acid accelerates the braising process and the tomatoes tie all the other ingredients together beautifully. Take the time and effort to cook it correctly, and each bite becomes a celebration of savory flavors. **Serves 4 to 6**

4 small veal shanks (10 to 12 ounces each, or 2 shanks if they are larger)
Kosher salt and freshly ground black pepper
1 cup all-purpose flour
³/₄ cup olive oil
1 yellow onion, diced
2 carrots, peeled and diced
1 celery stalk, diced
1 tablespoon tomato paste
1 cup good-quality red wine
3 cups chicken stock
One 28-ounce can crushed plum tomatoes
1 teaspoon dried thyme
¹/₂ teaspoon chopped fresh rosemary leaves
1 bay leaf
1 teaspoon prepared horseradish
Finely grated zest of 1 large lemon
2 tablespoons chopped fresh flat-leaf parsley

1. Preheat the oven to 350°F.
2. Pat the veal shanks dry with paper towels and then tie the meat to the bone with kitchen twine. Season each shank liberally with salt and pepper.
3. Spread the flour on a large plate. Dredge the shanks in the flour until they are coated all over. Shake off any excess and place the shanks on a clean plate.

4. In a large Dutch oven over medium-high heat, heat the oil. Add the veal shanks and brown on all sides. Transfer to a clean plate and set aside.

5. Add the onion, carrots, and celery to the pot and sauté until soft, about 5 minutes. Add the tomato paste and stir well until the vegetables are coated.

6. Add the wine and bring to a boil. Cook until reduced by half, about 2 minutes.

7. Add the stock, tomatoes, thyme, rosemary, bay leaf, horseradish, and veal shanks to the pot and bring to a boil. Transfer the pot to the oven and cook for 2 to 2½ hours, or until the meat is falling off the bone.

8. Transfer the shanks and vegetables to a serving platter. Remove and discard the bay leaf. Simmer the sauce in the pot over medium-high heat until it has reduced by one-quarter, 3 to 5 minutes. Taste and season with salt and pepper as needed.

9. Ladle the sauce over the veal shanks and sprinkle with the lemon zest and parsley. Serve alone, over creamy polenta, or with the Roasted Potatoes on page 173.

SAUSAGE, PEPPERS, AND ONIONS

It's difficult to improve upon the naturally wonderful spicy-sweet nature of sweet Italian sausage. Difficult, but not impossible—the key is to add a rainbow of bell peppers and cook up a nice, thick sauce to dress the peppers and onions. This dish makes spectacular use of traditional Italian herbs such as basil and oregano, which complement and bring out the subtler flavors in the sausage. Try not to change the ingredient amounts listed here. The uninitiated tend to skimp on the peppers, but the dish is meant to be a true ensemble. When you slice the sausage on the plate, every forkful should contain some sausage, some peppers, and a coating of sauce. **Serves 4 to 6**

1 pound sweet Italian sausage links
¼ cup extra-virgin olive oil
2 yellow onions, sliced
1 large red bell pepper, seeded and sliced
1 large green bell pepper, seeded and sliced
3 large garlic cloves, chopped
1 teaspoon kosher salt
1 teaspoon freshly ground black pepper
½ teaspoon dried oregano
3 tablespoons chopped fresh basil
1 tablespoon chopped fresh flat-leaf parsley
¼ teaspoon crushed red pepper flakes
½ cup good-quality dry red wine

1. Preheat the oven to 375°F.
2. Place the sausages on a rimmed baking sheet and bake for 25 to 30 minutes, turning once. The sausages should be browned and cooked through.
3. In a large, heavy skillet over medium heat, heat the olive oil. Add the onions and bell peppers and cook, stirring occasionally, until the onions soften and begin to brown.
4. Add the garlic and cook for 2 minutes. Add the salt, black pepper, and oregano and stir until the vegetables are coated in the spices.

5. Add the basil, parsley, and red pepper flakes and stir to combine. Add the wine and cook until the liquid has reduced by half, about 12 minutes.

6. Slice each sausage diagonally into thirds. Add the sausage to the skillet and cook until heated through. Serve hot, family style, on a platter.

A **NEW YORK** CLASSIC

Eat our Sausage, Peppers, and Onions alone, and they're divine. But you can pretend you live in Brooklyn like Frank Reagan does, and enjoy the dish Brooklyn style—on a hoagie roll or ciabatta bread. Brush a little olive oil on the cut faces of the bread, toast them face-down on a grill or in a skillet for about 1 minute, and then scoop the sausage, peppers, and onions onto the bottom of the roll. Clamp down the top, and enjoy a New York gem—the sausage-and-peppers grinder.

CROWN ROAST **OF** LAMB

It's the rare holiday table centerpiece that can rival the over-the-top impression of a properly cooked and served crown roast. It's meant to look just like a crown and the presentation is almost as stunning as the flavors. Although it's easy to find directions for cutting, Frenching (trimming meat from the ends of the rib bones for the unique "crown" appearance), and tying the roast, we recommend you have a butcher do this. Given the expense of two racks of lamb, you want the dish to look as wonderful as possible, and it's easy to mess up the preparation. A reputable butcher will prepare the crown roast for free if you buy it from him. Looks aside, you and your guests will enjoy the subtle, sweet delight of medium-rare lamb, an elegant meat like no other.

Serves 6 to 8

ROAST

One 4-pound crown roast (two 2-pound racks of ribs, chine cracked, tied, and ribs Frenched by the butcher—12 to 16 ribs)
1/4 cup extra-virgin olive oil
6 garlic cloves, minced
1/4 cup chopped fresh rosemary leaves
2 teaspoons kosher salt
1 teaspoon freshly ground black pepper

SAUCE

2 tablespoons extra-virgin olive oil
2 large shallots, minced
1/4 cup good-quality red wine
2 large sprigs fresh thyme
2 tablespoons cold unsalted butter, cut into 2 pats
Kosher salt and freshly ground black pepper

1. Preheat the oven to 400°F.
2. Make the roast: Coat the roast all over with the olive oil. In a small bowl, mix the garlic, rosemary, salt, and pepper until completely combined. Pat the rub all over the lamb. Cover the exposed bones with aluminum foil.

3. Roast the lamb for about 30 minutes, or until the internal temperature registers 130°F on an instant-read thermometer. Remove, reserve the pan juices, and tent with aluminum foil. Let the roast rest for 15 to 20 minutes.

4. While the roast is resting, make the sauce: Heat the olive oil in a saucepan. Add the shallots and sauté until they are soft and pick up some color. Add the red wine, thyme, and the reserved pan juices from the roast. Bring to a boil and cook until thickened to the consistency of syrup, about 8 minutes.

5. Remove the sauce from the heat and remove and discard the thyme sprigs. Whisk in the cold butter, one pat at a time. Taste and season with salt and pepper as needed.

6. Transfer the sauce to a sauceboat. Transfer the roast to a serving platter and remove the aluminum foil covering the bones. Place the stuffing or vegetables in the center of the roast and serve with the sauce.

VEAL SCALLOPINI

*Slice a lean meat like veal thinly and you wind up with exceedingly tender pieces. The problem is that the meat is prone to drying out. So what better way to keep that delicate meat moist, and maintain its lovely, buttery flavor, than to dress it in a light coating and bathe it in a silky butter-and-wine sauce? Even though scallopini is the height of simplicity to prepare and cook, you wouldn't know it from the elegant and enchanting presentation it makes. A sprinkle of parsley and a glass of nice Barolo are the only additions you'll need for this dish to be a truly memorable meal. **Serves 4***

½ cup all-purpose flour
1 teaspoon dried oregano
Kosher salt and freshly ground black pepper
1 pound veal scallopini (or use veal cutlets pounded thinner than ¼ inch)
¼ cup canola oil
4 tablespoons (½ stick) cold unsalted butter, cubed
2 tablespoons marsala wine
2 tablespoons capers, drained
1 tablespoon chopped fresh flat-leaf parsley

1. In a small bowl, whisk together the flour and oregano and season liberally with salt and pepper. Dredge the cutlets in the flour, coating them all over. Shake off any excess flour and transfer the cutlets to a clean plate.
2. Heat the oil in a large skillet over high heat. Working in batches, fry each cutlet until golden brown, about 1½ minutes per side. Transfer to a clean plate.
3. Drain the oil from the skillet and reduce the heat to medium. Add the butter and stir until it has melted. When the butter begins to brown, stir in the marsala and capers. Taste and add salt and pepper as needed.
4. Return the veal to the skillet and cook until heated through, about 3 minutes. Arrange the veal on a serving plate and dress with the sauce. Sprinkle with the parsley and serve.

BLUE **BLOODS** KITCHEN **TIP**

An instant-read thermometer is an essential tool for preparing meat or poultry in the kitchen. Of course, you have to know what temperature you're after before the thermometer can do you any good. Here are the temperatures pros use for different degrees of doneness for red meats (poultry should always be cooked to 165°F).

Rare	125°F (plus a 5-minute rest)
Medium-Rare	130°F plus rest
Medium	135°F plus rest
Medium-Well	145°F
Well	155°F+
Ground Beef	Always 160°F

GRILLED T-BONE STEAKS

*The T-bone is considered the king of steaks and is a favorite of guys like Tom Selleck—and the man he plays, Frank Reagan—thanks to its deep, pure beef flavor. Taken from the tenderest area of the animal, the T-bone is actually two steaks in one: a strip loin on the larger side, and tenderloin on the smaller side. The signature bone helps distribute heat and ensures that the meat cooks evenly and stays perfectly moist. The wonderful thing about high-quality cuts of beef such as the T-bone is that you really don't need to do much more than season the meat for it to come out perfectly. You do, however, have to grill it correctly if you want to make the most of your T-bone. **Serves 4**

> Two 1½ pound T-bone steaks (Prime grade if you can find them, but no less than Choice—look for steaks 2 inches thick)
> Kosher salt and coarsely ground black pepper

1. Preheat a grill on high, with burners or an area of the grill kept at medium (or use a grill pan large enough for hot and cool zones).
2. Let the steaks sit, unrefrigerated, for 30 minutes before cooking. After 15 minutes, pat them dry and coat with salt and pepper. The pepper will help establish the sear crust, so apply it thickly if you don't have a problem with the flavor of the pepper.
3. Sear the steaks over the hot area of the grill, flipping them as soon as they are seared on the bottoms. When both sides are seared, move the steaks to the cooler part of the grill to finish cooking. Total cooking time should be 10 to 12 minutes for medium-rare.
4. Check the steaks with an instant-read thermometer, being careful to avoid hitting the bone. Remove the steaks when they register 130°F, or medium-rare. (Or cook longer to your desired degree of doneness.)
5. Allow the steaks to rest for 10 minutes. Slice both sides of each steak away from the bone, and cut each section into ½-inch slices perpendicular to the bone. Reassemble the steaks around the bones, and serve immediately. (Or make it easier on yourself and go with a simpler presentation of the meat slices shingled on a serving platter.)

ARTHUR AVENUE SPAGHETTI AND MEATBALLS

Long before New York's Little Italy became famous for its cuisine, Italian immigrants living in the Bronx made Arthur Avenue famous for its Italian specialty shops and delis. The meatballs cooked there were the stuff of legend. We've captured that magic in these perfect orbs full of garlic, herbs, and the holy trinity of meats. The combination of ground veal, pork, and beef creates a flavor mix that far surpasses any of them alone. A few simple spices, a kiss of cheese, and a healthy dose of our own homemade marinara are all that you'll need to realize the ideal meatballs that would make the old souls on Arthur Avenue proud. This recipe makes a lot of meatballs and they freeze well, so don't be afraid to make the dish even if your crowd is small. You should serve the meal family style—on a large platter from which everybody serves themselves. **Serves 6 to 8**

1½ cups panko bread crumbs

3 cups chicken stock

2 large garlic cloves, minced

2 large eggs, beaten

2 tablespoons chopped fresh flat-leaf parsley

2 tablespoons chopped fresh basil

½ teaspoon dried oregano

2 teaspoons kosher salt

½ teaspoon freshly ground black pepper

½ pound ground veal

½ pound ground pork

½ pound ground beef (80% lean)

1 cup grated Parmesan cheese

6 cups Marinara like Mom Used to Make (page 248, or substitute your favorite jarred variety)

1½ pounds spaghetti, cooked al dente

1. Preheat the oven to 450°F.
2. In a large bowl, combine the bread crumbs, ¾ cup of the stock, the garlic, eggs,

1 tablespoon of the parsley, 1 tablespoon of the basil, the oregano, salt, and pepper.

3. Add the meats and ¾ cup of the Parmesan. Using your hands, mix well, but do not overwork. Refrigerate for 1 hour to allow the mixture to set up.

4. Lightly grease a high-sided baking pan with olive oil. Coat your hands with olive oil and form handball-size meatballs from the meat mixture. Space the meatballs evenly on the pan. Pour the remaining 2¼ cups stock into the pan and bake the meatballs for 15 to 20 minutes, or until they are nicely browned and cooked through. Remove from the oven.

5. Meanwhile, in a large pot, bring the marinara to a simmer. Transfer the meatballs to the pot with the marinara and keep warm.

6. To serve, add a ladleful of the sauce to the hot pasta in a large bowl and toss to completely coat the pasta. Add more sauce to thoroughly coat the noodles, but not so much that it pools. Spread the pasta out on a deep serving platter. Top with a modest amount of the sauce and the meatballs. Garnish with the remaining 1 tablespoon parsley, 1 tablespoon basil, and ¼ cup grated Parmesan. Serve with the remaining sauce on the side.

SANDWICH OPTIONS

Leftover meatballs are like the pot of gold at the end of leprechaun's rainbow—hard to come by and mighty valuable. The best use in the world for leftover meatballs is that East Coast favorite of favorites, the meatball grinder. Also known as a "hoagie" or "hero," this is an easy sandwich to throw together, but one that creates an over-the-moon eating experience. Simply split a hoagie roll lengthwise and lay down a thick coating of marinara sauce on the bottom half of the roll. Lovingly nestle three warm meatballs, side by side, in this bed, and cover with thin slices of mozzarella. Heat the sandwich in a preheated 450°F oven until the cheese has completely melted. Clamp down the top half of the hoagie roll and let the feast begin!

STUFFED SALMON

You don't have to be a fish fanatic to love salmon. The sturdy flavor of the fish is unlike anything else a fisherman reels in, at once light, memorable, and delectable. As wonderful as it is all by itself, salmon really becomes something special when you stuff it with a combination of garden-fresh goodness, a bit of white wine, and the decadence of melt-in-your-mouth shrimp. The hardest part of this recipe is cutting the pocket for the stuffing; it's best done with slow, careful movements and a very sharp paring knife. Once cooked and served, you're sure to wish—as we do—that salmon were reeled in stuffed.

Serves 4

Four 8- to 10-ounce center-cut salmon fillets
Kosher salt and freshly ground black pepper
3 tablespoons olive oil
½ shallot, minced
2 cremini mushrooms, stems removed, cleaned, and finely diced
¼ pound medium to large shrimp, cleaned and chopped
½ cup fresh spinach, chopped
2 tablespoons dry white wine
¼ cup panko bread crumbs
Finely grated zest of 2 lemons
1 lemon, cut into wedges

1. Season the salmon all over with salt and pepper. Cut a pocket in the top of each fillet, being careful not to cut all the way through.
2. In a large sauté pan over medium-high heat, heat 2 tablespoons of the olive oil. Add the shallot and cook just until it starts to soften. Add the mushrooms and cook until they begin to brown.
3. Add the shrimp and season liberally with salt and pepper. Cook until opaque and pink, about 2 minutes. Add the white wine and stir to deglaze the pan, scraping up any browned bits from the bottom of the pan.
4. Remove the pan from the heat and add the spinach. Let it cook just until it begins to wilt, 1 to 2 minutes. Add the bread crumbs and stir in.
5. Preheat the broiler.

6. Stuff the salmon pockets with the stuffing. Wipe out the pan and add the remaining 1 tablespoon olive oil. Return the pan to the burner over medium-high heat.

7. Place the stuffed salmon in the pan, skin-side down, and cook for 1 minute. Lower the heat to medium-low and cook for about 5 minutes, or until the salmon is opaque and cooked to desired doneness. (Depending on the size of the pan, you may have to cook the fish in batches.)

8. Transfer the fillets to a nonstick baking sheet and broil for 1 to 2 minutes until the top turns golden brown. Top each fillet with a sprinkling of lemon zest. Serve with a lemon wedge.

THE ULTIMATE, OVER-THE-TOP, ODE-TO-DANNY-REAGAN BACON CHEESEBURGER

Much as holes are to the Grand Canyon, there are cheeseburgers, and then there is this incredible creation. It is greater than the sum of its parts, but you can feel free to do without any single part except the burger and bun. We recommend you go for the total experience though. You won't soon forget it. That's because the burger is made with exceptional sirloin rather than the more pedestrian ground chuck, and kept moist with butter. (You'll rarely go wrong when you start with butter!) We use our own special sauce, and build the burger with lush sautéed onions and a helping of bacon. **Serves 4**

ONIONS (OPTIONAL)
2 tablespoons unsalted butter

1 tablespoon olive oil

1 yellow onion, thinly sliced

BURGER
1½ pounds sirloin steak, cubed

Kosher salt and freshly ground black pepper

1 teaspoon cold unsalted butter, cut into 4 equal pieces

4 strips thick-cut, high-quality bacon

4 thin slices sharp cheddar cheese (or substitute your favorite cheese)

4 potato buns

SAUCE
¼ cup real mayonnaise

2 tablespoons ketchup

2 tablespoons Dijon mustard

1 teaspoon Worcestershire sauce

1 teaspoon finely minced fresh dill

1 teaspoon fresh lemon juice

Dash of Tabasco sauce

1. Make the onions (if using): Heat the butter and oil over medium-low heat. Add the onions and cook, turning occasionally, for about 45 minutes, or until completely soft and brown.

2. Make the burgers: Put the sirloin cubes and your mixer grinder attachment in the freezer, just until the outside of the meat is hard but the inside remains soft, 10 to 15 minutes. Grind the cubes through your mixer attachment, or in a food processor. Grind it coarse. (You can also just have your butcher grind sirloin fresh for you, but cook it the same day.)

3. Let the ground sirloin come to room temperature. Season the meat liberally with salt and pepper. Wash your hands and mix the meat with the seasoning, then form 4 equal patties. Make the patties as wide as the buns, but don't overwork them.

4. Push a piece of the cold butter into the center of each patty. Cover up the hole so that the butter is sealed inside the patty.

5. Preheat a grill or grill pan over medium-high heat. Preheat the oven to 425°F.

6. Cut the strips of bacon in half crosswise. Line a baking sheet with parchment paper, and crisscross each of the cut bacon slices to make an X shape on the parchment paper. Cover with a sheet of parchment paper and cook in the preheated oven for 12 to 15 minutes until crisp.

7. Grill the burgers for about 4 minutes each side, flipping them only once. The internal temperature should register about 135°F for medium (although the USDA recommends 160°F—well done—for ground meat to eliminate risk of bacteria). When the burgers have about 2 minutes to cook on the second side, put a slice of cheese on each burger.

8. Remove the burgers from the grill and let rest for 5 minutes.

9. While the burgers rest, make the sauce: Combine all the sauce ingredients in a small bowl and whisk together until evenly colored throughout.

10. Assemble the burgers: Butter the face of each bun and toast them on the grill for about 1 minute.

11. Set a patty on each bun bottom, top with a tablespoon of sauce, a bacon X, the onions (if using), and the top of the bun. Serve immediately.

BEHIND THE SCENES . . . **WITH WENDY**

Tom Selleck has a reputation in the industry as a meticulous, dedicated actor. So it was no surprise that when he first took on the character of Reagan family—and NYPD—patriarch Frank Reagan, he wanted to dive as deeply as possible into the character. He even asked one of the show's writers to write a detailed biography of Frank. Where did he go to high school? Where was he born? Facts like that. He wanted to know every detail, including what Frank had done to earn each of the medals on his character's dress uniform. To this day, if you ask Tom about a specific medal he wears, he can tell you how Frank earned it!

PASTA PRIMAVERA

Splitting the difference between a fresh pasta salad and roasted vegetables, this pasta primavera is a vegetarian delight that even carnivores will love. The cascade of bell peppers adds color, a beautiful presentation made even more vibrant with carrots and tomatoes. A simple olive oil dressing gives the pasta a touch of Italian style. We've used basic corkscrew (rotini) pasta for our primavera because the ridges hold the dressing and herbs like a sponge. But feel free to substitute your own favorite pasta—farfalle or orecchiette would work every bit as well. **Serves 4 to 6**

2 carrots, peeled and cut into matchsticks
1 large yellow bell pepper, seeded and chopped
1 large red bell pepper, seeded and chopped
1 large orange bell pepper, seeded and chopped
1 small red onion, thinly sliced
2 garlic cloves, chopped
1 zucchini, cut in half lengthwise and sliced into half-moons
¼ cup extra-virgin olive oil
1 teaspoon dried oregano
Kosher salt and freshly ground black pepper
12 ounces rotini pasta
2 tablespoons red wine vinegar
1 pint cherry tomatoes, halved
¼ cup grated Parmesan cheese

1. Preheat the oven to 450°F.
2. In a large bowl, combine the carrots, bell peppers, onion, garlic, and zucchini. In a small bowl, whisk together the olive oil and oregano. Season lightly with salt and black pepper and pour the mixture over the vegetables. Toss until the vegetables are completely coated.
3. Transfer the vegetables to a large baking sheet and spread them out in an even layer. Bake for 20 to 30 minutes, just until the carrots have softened and started to brown.
4. When the vegetables have about 5 minutes left to cook, bring a large pot of

heavily salted water to a boil over high heat. Cook the pasta until it is al dente and drain it.

5. Transfer the pasta to a large serving bowl and top with the warm vegetables, including any juices on the baking sheet. Drizzle with the vinegar and thoroughly mix the vegetables with the pasta, until the pasta is entirely coated.

6. Add the tomatoes, and gently mix them into the primavera. Taste and add salt and black pepper as needed. (Add 1 to 2 tablespoons olive oil if the pasta is too dry.) Dust with the Parmesan and serve immediately.

BROILED HALIBUT

*Halibut is a chef's favorite fish for the many ways it can be prepared and how well it showcases so many flavorings, from dense and sweet to tart and tangy. We prefer ours subtle and simple. A small scattering of herbs and a bit of citrus lend far more flavor than you might imagine, and they do it without adding calories. That's an important consideration for one of the healthiest dishes you would ever find in the Reagan household. The fish is low in fat, high in protein, and packed with heart-healthy omega-3 fatty acids and other compounds that help prevent disease. Delicious as it is, it's a guilt-free dinner. **Serves 4***

Four 6-ounce halibut fillets
Kosher salt and freshly ground black pepper
4 tablespoons (½ stick) unsalted butter
3 garlic cloves, minced
1 tablespoon dried parsley
1 teaspoon dried oregano
2 lemons: 1 cut into wedges and 1 thinly sliced
1 tablespoon chopped fresh flat-leaf parsley

1. Preheat the broiler. Grease a large baking dish.
2. Season the fish with salt and pepper and arrange the fillets in the baking dish.
3. In a small pot over low heat, combine the butter, garlic, dried parsley, oregano, and a light seasoning of salt and pepper. Heat until the butter has melted, and then cook for 5 minutes.
4. Carefully pour the butter mixture over the fish, coating each fillet. Broil for about 4 minutes on each side, flipping halfway through, until the fish flakes easily.
5. Transfer the fillets to individual plates. Line each fillet with lemon slices, and squeeze a lemon wedge over each. Sprinkle with the fresh parsley and serve.

SOUTHERN FRIED (BAKED) CHICKEN

Southern cooks and barbecue pitmasters might want to flip right past this page, because it's a bit of a Southern cooking sacrilege. But the fact is, deep-frying chicken requires a deep fryer or a big pot full of very hot oil. Either way, it's messy, smelly, and more than a little bit dangerous. It's also one of the more unhealthy ways to prepare food. The problem is, how to capture that deep-fried crusty crunch and the super-moist chicken meat that lies under it? The answer is to bread the chicken just like you would for frying, then bake it for a good long time. We use fine panko bread crumbs, but you can substitute crushed cornflakes for a slightly more authentically Southern texture.

Serves 4 to 6

8 assorted chicken pieces (include your preference of thighs, drumsticks, wings, and breasts, or break down 2 whole small fryers)
²/₃ cup all-purpose flour
Kosher salt and freshly ground black pepper

1 cup buttermilk
2 tablespoons Dijon mustard
½ teaspoon dried oregano
¼ teaspoon cayenne pepper
½ teaspoon smoked paprika
4 cups panko bread crumbs

1. Preheat the oven to 450°F. Rinse the chicken pieces and pat dry with paper towels.
2. In a small bowl, season the flour liberally with salt and pepper and whisk to combine. In a large bowl, combine the buttermilk, mustard, oregano, cayenne, and paprika. Stir until completely incorporated. Spread the bread crumbs on a plate.
3. Working one at a time, dredge each piece of chicken in the flour, shaking off the excess. Then dip it into the buttermilk, coating it thoroughly and letting any excess drip off. Then press the chicken into the bread crumbs. Roll it until it is completely coated. Repeat the dredging process with all the chicken pieces.
4. Put a wire rack on a baking sheet and space out the chicken evenly on the rack. Bake for 20 minutes, turn the chicken, and lower the oven temperature to 375°F. Bake for 45 minutes more, or until the surfaces of the chicken pieces are dark brown. The interior temperature of the chicken should register 165°F on an instant-read thermometer, and the juices should run clear when the meat is pierced.
5. Transfer to a wire rack and let rest for 5 to 10 minutes. Serve warm.

POT ROAST

*The goal of pot roast is to transform a large, inexpensive cut of meat into a fall-apart tender meal in a pot. It's achieved by a long cooking time and plenty of liquid, both of which also help flavor the meat. Combine the meat with some sturdy vegetables and a few spices, and you wind up with one of the most down-to-earth, completely satisfying meals you can put on a family dinner table. It's only made better by the fact that it's one of the simplest meals to make. **Serves 4***

One 4-pound beef chuck roast
Kosher salt and freshly ground black pepper
2 tablespoons olive oil
3 large garlic cloves, peeled and crushed
1 cup good-quality red wine
2 large yellow onions, quartered
4 large carrots, peeled and cut on the diagonal into 2-inch pieces
3 cups beef broth
3 sprigs fresh rosemary
3 sprigs fresh thyme
1 teaspoon dried oregano

1. Preheat the oven to 250°F.
2. Let the roast come to room temperature, then liberally season it all over with salt and pepper.
3. In a 6-quart Dutch oven over medium-high heat, heat the olive oil. Sear the roast on all sides, just until the surface is browned. Transfer to a clean plate.
4. Add the garlic to the pot and cook for 2 minutes. Add the wine and deglaze the pot, scraping up any browned bits on the bottom.
5. Return the roast to the pot and add the onions and carrots. Cover with the broth and add the rosemary, thyme, and oregano. Season lightly with salt and pepper, cover, and transfer the pot to the oven.
6. Braise for 3½ to 4 hours, or until you can pull the meat apart with a fork. Transfer the meat and vegetables to a serving platter (discard the herb sprigs) and serve hot.

FOUR-CHEESE MAC-AND-CHEESE

If one cheese is good, two is better. And if two is better, four is just downright fantastic. Though you may be a fan of the store-bought boxed variety that reminds you of your youth, we think this mac-and-cheese is about to change your mind. The cheeses here all have distinctively different flavors, but they meld like magic. You'll think you've discovered one brand-new super-delicious cheese! What's even better is that the dish comes together in a snap, making it a perfect busy-weeknight option. But it won't seem simple or rushed when it hits the table, with its alluring crispy coating and hunger-crushing cheese bubbling up from underneath. **Serves 4 to 6**

3 tablespoons unsalted butter
1 shallot, minced
3 tablespoons all-purpose flour
½ teaspoon kosher salt
¼ teaspoon freshly ground white pepper
¼ teaspoon smoked paprika
2 cups half-and-half
8 ounces Fontina cheese, shredded
4 ounces sharp cheddar cheese, shredded
4 ounces Swiss cheese, shredded
¼ cup grated Parmesan cheese
One 16-ounce package rotini pasta (or substitute your favorite corkscrew
   pasta or elbow macaroni), cooked al dente
⅔ cup panko bread crumbs

1. Preheat the oven to 350°F. Grease a 3-quart ovenproof casserole dish.
2. In a large pot over medium heat, melt the butter. Add the shallot and cook, stirring, until it softens, about 3 minutes. Add the flour, salt, white pepper, and paprika and whisk until combined.
3. Add the half-and-half and whisk until thickened, about 5 minutes. Remove from the heat. Add the cheeses and stir until the cheeses have melted. Add the pasta to the pot and stir to combine. Transfer to the prepared casserole dish. Spread the bread crumbs evenly over the pasta.
4. Bake the casserole for 20 minutes, or until the top is browned and crispy. Serve hot.

THE THANKSGIVING TURKEY

Cooking the perfect Thanksgiving turkey starts with buying the right bird. That starts with size. Most cooks overestimate the amount of turkey they need—even considering leftovers. Figure 1 pound for every person at the table, plus 5 pounds extra (for the parts that won't be eaten, and sandwiches later). Smaller turkeys are often the better choice. A turkey under 20 pounds is most likely a hen. Larger tom turkeys tend to be more muscular, which translates to tougher, often drier meat.

Most people buy a frozen turkey, although paying a bit more for a fresh turkey makes everything easier, because you don't have to thaw the bird. If you've opted for frozen, start defrosting the turkey several days before you cook it by moving it to the refrigerator. It will take about 24 hours for every 5 pounds. You can speed up the process, if need be, by thawing the bird in a large container full of cold water, changing the water every half hour. In either case, carefully inspect the vacuum bag around the turkey—it should be tight and sealed, with no leaks, holes, tears, bagging, or air pockets.

One turkey, fresh or frozen (see headnote)
1 cup (2 sticks) unsalted butter
Kosher salt and freshly ground black pepper
3 cups chicken broth

1. Remove the turkey from the refrigerator 20 to 30 minutes before you want to put it in the oven, and remove the package of giblets from the neck. (You can reserve these for homemade gravy if you like, or for other uses as well.)
2. Melt the butter and keep it warm.
3. Season the turkey all over with salt and pepper. Place the turkey in a large roasting pan equipped with a rack. If your pan doesn't have a rack, use 6 to 8 cut potato halves spaced evenly in the bottom of the pan, cut-side down (or use celery stalks or large carrots). You don't want the bottom of the turkey cooking in its own juices. Pour the chicken broth into the pan.
4. Preheat the oven to 450°F.
5. Put the turkey in the preheated oven and then lower the oven temperature to 375°F. Assume 15 minutes per pound for the cooking time, and baste the turkey

every 20 to 30 minutes, first with the juices from the roasting pan, and then with the melted butter for the last two times.

6. Once the skin has browned, cover the top of the bird with aluminum foil to prevent it from charring. Remove the turkey from the oven when an instant-read thermometer stuck into the thickest part of the thigh meat registers 165°F.

7. Let the bird rest for 20 to 30 minutes before carving. To carve, remove the wings, drumsticks, thighs, and breasts. Carve the meat off the turkey for best results, and arrange it on a serving platter to bring to the table. Always refrigerate leftovers within 2 hours, to keep the meat food safe.

SOLE PICCATA

This is a remarkably versatile recipe that is ideal for dressing up this simple fish, or even flounder or tilapia (you can even sub in chicken!). The recipe is simple and quick, and it takes the guesswork out of cooking a delicate fish that is prone to drying out. Although you are panfrying the fish, the flavors remain a refined balance between salty and tangy. The velvety sauce ties the whole dish together. Just be sure to collect and assemble all the ingredients before you start, because the cooking moves along fairly quickly.

Serves 4

Four 6-ounce sole fillets (we recommend Dover or grey sole)
Kosher salt and freshly ground black pepper
½ cup all-purpose flour
1 tablespoon olive oil
3 tablespoons unsalted butter
⅓ cup dry white wine
Juice of 1 lemon
2 tablespoons capers, drained
1 tablespoon chopped fresh flat-leaf parsley

1. Season the fish on both sides with salt and pepper. Spread the flour on a wide shallow plate and dredge each fillet until it is completely coated. Shake off any excess flour and transfer the fillets to a clean plate.
2. Heat a large saucepan over medium–high heat. Add the olive oil and 2 tablespoons of the butter.
3. When the butter has completely melted and is beginning to brown, add the fish fillets (working in batches of two, if necessary). Cook the fish fillets until brown on the bottom, then flip and cook until golden brown on the undersides, about 2 minutes per side. Transfer the fillets to four individual dinner plates.
4. Add the wine and deglaze the pan, scraping up any browned bits from the bottom. Add the lemon juice and capers and stir to combine. Cook for 1 minute, remove the pan from the heat, then add the remaining 1 tablespoon butter and whisk it into the sauce.
5. Dress the fillets with the sauce, being careful not to oversauce the fish. Sprinkle parsley over the top of each plate and serve.

IRISH STEW

To understand Irish stew, you have to understand the weather of Ireland. Much of the country is draped in a damp cold that seeps right into your bones, so a robust stew is essential to warm a body from the inside out. Immigrants like the Reagans—especially Irish beat cops—found similar weather in the coastal town of Manhattan and turned to the stew to take the chill out of a bitter night. Of course, you don't need the excuse of bad weather to enjoy the toasty broth, fork-tender vegetables, and flavor-soaked meat in this recipe. Traditional Irish stew was likely to include mutton, but the gamey taste can be a little off-putting, so we've used beef in our stew. Keep the recipe handy for the next time a storm blows in. **Serves 6**

1 pound cubed beef stew meat (preferably from the shoulder)
Kosher salt and freshly ground black pepper
4 tablespoons (1/2 stick) unsalted butter
3 Russet potatoes, peeled and cubed
1 yellow onion, chopped
4 carrots, peeled and chopped
2 tablespoons canola oil
4 large garlic cloves, minced
1 1/2 tablespoons tomato paste
1 teaspoon sugar
1 tablespoon dried thyme
1/2 teaspoon dried savory
1 tablespoon Worcestershire sauce
2 cups Guinness draught beer (not stout)
4 cups beef stock
1 bay leaf
2 tablespoons chopped fresh flat-leaf parsley

1. Let the meat come to room temperature, then season it with salt and pepper.
2. In a 6-quart Dutch oven over medium-high heat, melt the butter. Add the potatoes, onion, and carrots and cook, stirring frequently, for about 7 minutes, or until the vegetables have softened slightly. Transfer the vegetables to a large bowl and set aside.

3. Heat the oil in the Dutch oven over medium-high heat. Add the meat and brown on all sides.

4. Add the garlic and cook for 1 minute. Add the tomato paste and cook, stirring, until the meat is well coated and the paste is just about to caramelize, about 2 minutes.

5. Add the sugar, thyme, savory, and Worcestershire sauce and season lightly with salt and pepper. Pour in the beer and deglaze the pot, scraping up any browned bits on the bottom.

6. Add the stock and bay leaf and bring to a boil. Reduce the heat and simmer for 1 hour, or until the liquid has reduced by one-quarter and thickened.

7. Remove and discard the bay leaf. Add the cooked vegetables and simmer for 20 minutes. Sprinkle the parsley over the top of the stew and serve hot, with Irish Soda Bread (page 197).

EGGPLANT PARMESAN

*We have Amy Carlson to thank for this recipe. Amy plays Linda Reagan, the wife of Don-
nie Wahlberg's character, Detective Danny Reagan, on* Blue Bloods. *The recipe hasn't
yet made an appearance on the show, but it should. The secret to Amy's version is a
frying method that will save burns, grease cleanup, and splatters around the kitchen.
Even though it's a little unorthodox, it fries the eggplant perfectly, making the homemade breading delightfully crunchy. In the process, the eggplant itself becomes tender
and moist, the ideal in any eggplant Parmesan.* **Serves 6 to 8**

2 medium eggplants, trimmed and cut crosswise into ¼-inch slices

3 tablespoons kosher salt, plus ¼ teaspoon

8 slices good-quality white bread, torn into small pieces

1½ cups grated Parmesan cheese

1½ teaspoons freshly ground black pepper

1 cup all-purpose flour

4 large eggs, beaten

6 tablespoons canola oil

2 tablespoons extra-virgin olive oil

4 garlic cloves, minced

¼ teaspoon crushed red pepper flakes

Three 14.5-ounce cans crushed tomatoes

One 14.5-ounce can diced tomatoes

¾ cup fresh basil leaves, chopped

One 12-ounce bag shredded mozzarella

1. In a large bowl, toss the eggplant slices with the 3 tablespoons salt until all the
   slices are well coated. Transfer to a colander set over a large bowl and set aside to
   drain for 30 to 45 minutes, or until the eggplant releases about 2 tablespoons of
   liquid.
2. While the eggplant is draining, preheat the oven to 425°F. Position the racks in
   the center of the oven and put one baking sheet on each rack.
3. Pulse the bread in a food processor into fine crumbs. Transfer the crumbs to a
   large bowl. Add 1 cup of the Parmesan cheese, the remaining ¼ teaspoon salt,

and ½ teaspoon of the black pepper. Transfer to a pie plate (or divide between two, as necessary).

4. Combine the flour and the remaining 1 teaspoon black pepper in a 1-gallon resealable freezer bag. Shake until the flour and pepper are completely mixed. Put the beaten eggs in a shallow pie plate.

5. Pat the eggplant slices dry with paper towels and wipe off any excess salt.

6. Working in batches, add the slices to the freezer bag with the flour mixture. Seal the bag and shake until the slices are coated in flour. Remove the eggplant and shake off any excess flour. Repeat with all the slices.

7. Dip each slice in the egg until thoroughly coated. Let any excess drip off. Press the slice into the bread crumb mixture until coated on all sides. Shake off any excess and transfer the eggplant to a wire rack. Repeat with all the slices.

8. Remove the preheated baking sheet from the oven and add 3 tablespoons of the canola oil to each pan, tilting to coat evenly.

9. Place half of the eggplant slices on each sheet in a single layer and put the pans in the oven. Switch and rotate the sheet after 10 minutes of baking. Flip the eggplant slices after 20 minutes. Bake until well browned and crisp, about 35 minutes.

10. While the eggplant bakes, combine the olive oil, garlic, and red pepper flakes in a large saucepan over medium-high heat. Cook, stirring frequently, until the garlic is light golden, about 5 minutes.

11. Stir in the crushed and diced tomatoes, increase the heat to high, and bring the sauce to a boil. Reduce the heat to a simmer and cook, stirring occasionally, until thickened and reduced, about 15 minutes. Stir in ½ cup of the chopped basil. Taste and add salt and black pepper as needed.

12. Spread about 1 cup of the sauce in the bottom of a 9 x 13-inch baking dish. Cover with half the eggplant slices, shingling them as necessary to fit. Cover with about 1 cup of the sauce and about half the shredded mozzarella.

13. Repeat with the remaining ingredients (reserve a bit of the mozzarella for sprinkling on top), dotting the top layer of eggplant with sauce, so it will be exposed and remain crisp. Sprinkle with the remaining ½ cup Parmesan and any the reserved mozzarella.

14. Bake until the sauce is bubbling and the cheese is slightly browned, about 15 minutes. Cool for 10 minutes. Scatter the remaining basil over the top and serve warm, with any remaining sauce on the side.

LASAGNA

There are many ways to put a new spin on this long-treasured pasta classic, and all have to do with what is used in the layers. We love sweet Italian sausage, so that was a natural meat for us to choose when it came time to build the lasagna. We also added roasted red peppers for their tempting texture and slightly sharp flavor. A mixture of four tra- ditional cheeses and a touch of basil rounds out our version. Keep in mind that this is absolutely an ideal make-ahead main course that can be refrigerated for two days, or frozen for weeks before cooking. **Serves 6 to 8**

One 1-pound box lasagna noodles
2 tablespoons olive oil
1 large yellow onion, diced
2 garlic cloves, minced
1 teaspoon dried oregano
¾ pound loose sweet Italian sausage
¾ pound ground beef
6 cups Marinara like Mom Used to Make (page 248)
Kosher salt and freshly ground black pepper
2 pounds whole-milk ricotta cheese
1 large egg
¼ cup grated Pecorino Romano cheese
¼ cup chopped fresh basil
1 pound mozzarella cheese, shredded
1 cup roasted red peppers
1 cup grated Parmesan cheese

1. Preheat the oven to 375°F. Coat a baking sheet with olive oil.
2. Fill a large pot with water, salt heavily, and bring to a boil over high heat. Boil the noodles for 6 to 8 minutes, or just until pliable but not cooked through. Drain and set aside in a single layer on the baking sheet.
3. In a large pot, heat the olive oil over medium-high heat. Add the onion and garlic and cook until the onion softens, about 3 minutes.

4. Add the oregano, sausage, and beef and cook until the meat is completely browned, about 10 minutes. Drain off any excess grease. Add 3 cups of the marinara sauce, season lightly with salt and black pepper, and bring to a simmer.

5. In a large bowl, combine the ricotta, egg, Pecorino Romano, and basil. Stir with a fork until completely incorporated. Set aside.

6. Coat the bottom of a 9 x 13-inch baking dish or lasagna pan with marinara sauce. Cover with a layer of noodles. Top with about one-third of the meat sauce and one-third of the mozzarella.

7. Repeat with a second layer, and top with another third of the mozzarella and the roasted red peppers.

8. Repeat with a third layer, and top with the remaining mozzarella and the grated Parmesan.

9. Bake the lasagna in the center of the oven for 45 to 50 minutes, or until the sauce is bubbling around the edges and the top is beginning to brown. Let rest for at least 10 minutes before cutting and serving.

BEEF STROGANOFF

This is a dish with history. The original dates back, in one form or another, to seventeenth-century Russia. You only get that kind of longevity in something truly delicious, and in this case, truly delicious means super-tender meat bathed in a delectable sour cream sauce. The meat and luscious sauce are traditionally served over egg noodles, and we've stuck to tradition. The combination of thick sauce, beef, and dense noodles makes for a very filling meal. Tailor the recipe to the number of people you're serving because for all its other virtues, beef stroganoff does not make for stellar leftovers.

Serves 4 to 6

1½ pounds beef tenderloin
Kosher salt and freshly ground black pepper
2 tablespoons canola oil
4 tablespoons (½ stick) unsalted butter
1 yellow onion, diced
1 pound white button mushrooms, stems trimmed, thickly sliced
2 tablespoons all-purpose flour
1½ cups beef broth
2 tablespoons Dijon mustard
1 cup sour cream
3 tablespoons minced fresh flat-leaf parsley
One 12-ounce bag egg noodles, cooked al dente
2 tablespoons chopped fresh flat-leaf parsley

1. Remove the meat from the refrigerator, trim the fat, and cut the meat into strips each about ½ inch thick. Allow the meat to come to room temperature. Season lightly all over with salt and pepper.
2. In a large skillet with high sides, heat the oil over high heat. Sear the meat strips in batches, about 2 minutes per side. The meat should be just seared, but not releasing juices. Transfer to a clean plate and set aside.
3. Reduce the heat to medium and add the butter. As soon as the butter melts, add the onion and sauté for about 3 minutes, or just until beginning to soften.
4. Add the mushrooms and cook until soft and browned, 10 to 12 minutes. Add the flour and stir to coat the vegetables.

5. While the mushrooms are cooking, combine the broth, mustard, and sour cream in a medium bowl. Whisk until smooth.

6. Stir the broth mixture into the cooked mushrooms and bring to a simmer; do not allow the mixture to boil. Add the meat and simmer for about 5 minutes, or until the sauce thickens and the meat is heated through.

7. Add the noodles to the pan for the final 2 minutes of cooking and toss to coat with the sauce. Sprinkle the parsley over the top and serve hot.

FLANK STEAK

*Cooking a great flank steak begins with buying a great flank steak. Look for a bright red color and ample marbling (streaks of fat), both of which point to tenderness in what is classically a very tough—but super-flavorful—piece of meat. That toughness is why you must marinate before cooking. We prefer a slightly Asian style of marinade, with a little sweetness cut by salt and acidity. Substitute your own favorite marinade if you prefer. Cooking the steak is easy; the most important part of the process is letting it rest long enough so that the juices evenly saturate the meat. Then cut it against—at a right angle to—the fibers of the meat, which are clearly visible as strands. **Serves 4 to 6**time*

2 garlic cloves, peeled and crushed
Finely grated zest and juice of 2 lemons
2 tablespoons soy sauce
1 teaspoon peeled and minced fresh ginger
1 teaspoon kosher salt
$\frac{1}{2}$ teaspoon freshly ground black pepper
1 teaspoon brown sugar
One 2-pound flank steak

1. In a large bowl with a lid, combine the garlic, lemon zest, lemon juice, soy sauce, ginger, salt, pepper, and brown sugar. Whisk until entirely incorporated.
2. Add the steak to the marinade and turn to coat. Cover and refrigerate for 1 hour and up to several hours, turning every 20 minutes.
3. Preheat a grill or grill pan over high heat. Heat separate burners or a separate area of the grill with medium heat (or raise the grill over one section to be further from the heat source).
4. Remove the steak from the marinade and pat dry with paper towels. Let the meat come to room temperature. Grill it over high heat for about 4 minutes per side, until the outside is seared and charred with grill marks.
5. Move the steak to medium heat. Cook for about 3 minutes more per side, or until an instant-read thermometer registers 130°F. Transfer the steak to a cutting board and let rest for 10 minutes. Cut into thin slices against the grain and serve.

SIDES

ROASTED POTATOES

*Families with the background of the Reagans would consider this a favorite for the way it dresses up plain old spuds. Sprinkle cut potatoes with a shower of shredded hard cheese and rosemary, and you elevate them to something else. Once roasted, the combination creates contrasting yet complementary textures. The creamy potatoes play against the crunchy saltiness of the Parmesan in a perfect way. A dusting of sturdy rosemary is the ideal capper to the combination, accenting the flavors of both the cheese and potatoes. Be warned that more than one family member may try to make this the main course of the meal—so make extra. **Serves 4 to 6***

⅓ cup olive oil
Kosher salt and freshly ground black pepper
2 tablespoons finely chopped fresh rosemary leaves (from about 2 large sprigs)
Juice of 1 small lemon
1 garlic clove, minced
2 pounds small red potatoes, scrubbed
¼ cup shredded Parmesan cheese, or more as desired

1. Preheat the oven to 400°F.
2. In a large bowl, combine the olive oil, salt and pepper to taste, rosemary, lemon juice, and garlic. Whisk to thoroughly mix.
3. Cut the potatoes in half (quarter if large) and add to the bowl. Toss to completely coat the potatoes.
4. Arrange the potatoes, cut-side up, on a wire rack, set on a baking sheet. (If you don't have a rack, roast the potatoes on the baking sheet, turning them twice during the cooking.)
5. Roast the potatoes for 20 minutes. Remove from the oven and sprinkle with the Parmesan. Return to the oven and roast for 15 minutes more, or until the cut surfaces begin to brown and a knife easily penetrates a potato. Serve hot.

ROASTED GARLIC STUFFING

Stuffing—especially this one—isn't just for holidays. Infused with the dreamy savory-sweet richness of roasted garlic, this side could be right at home on just about any family dinner table. The twist is just a dash of crunch and tang courtesy of Granny Smith apples. The flavor of the apple ever so slightly cuts the opulence of the roasted garlic, creating a wonderful contrast on the tongue. Serve this with chicken or lighter meats such as pork, and don't be surprised when it becomes your go-to stuffing for those fancy holiday affairs! **Serves 6**

1 loaf French bread (to make 4 cups croutons)
8 tablespoons (1 stick) unsalted butter
1 cup diced Vidalia onion
$^2/_3$ cup diced celery
1 cup peeled, cored and diced Granny Smith apple
2 cups chicken stock
2 tablespoons Roasted Garlic (page 250)
1 teaspoon chopped fresh thyme leaves
2 tablespoons chopped fresh chives
2 tablespoons chopped fresh basil

1. Preheat the oven to 425°F.
2. Slice the bread. Tear the slices into small pieces, about the size of a nickel. Spread out the pieces on a baking sheet. Bake for about 30 minutes, or until brown and dry. Remove the bread and reduce the oven temperature to 375°F.
3. In a large pot over medium heat, melt the butter. Add the onion, celery, and apple and cook until the onion is soft, about 3 minutes.
4. Add the stock and simmer until the liquid has reduced by about half. Add the garlic, thyme, chives, and basil and stir to completely combine. Add the croutons and stir until all the croutons are wet.
5. Transfer the stuffing to a 2-quart ovenproof baking dish. Bake for 30 to 40 minutes, or until golden brown on top. Serve warm.

SAUTÉED LEEKS

Sure, this side dish sounds simple and it is. But easy as it is to make, it is a subtle combination of powerful flavors. Those flavors are woven together and tempered to make for an intriguing and compelling taste sensation that really wakes up your taste buds. The secret is the peppercorns, which slightly numb the tongue and prevent any one flavor from overwhelming the others. Word to the wise: Thoroughly wash the leeks before cooking, because even the slightest bit of leftover grit can ruin the dish. **Serves 4**

2 tablespoons extra-virgin olive oil
4 large leeks (white part only), cut on the diagonal into 1-inch slices
1 teaspoon tricolored peppercorns
1 teaspoon chopped fresh rosemary leaves
½ teaspoon kosher salt
1 cup vegetable broth
Finely grated zest and juice of 1 small lemon

1. In a large saucepan over medium-high heat, heat the olive oil. Add the leeks and peppercorns and cook until the leeks are lightly browned, tossing occasionally.
2. Add the rosemary and salt and cook, stirring, for 1 minute. Add the broth, lemon zest, and lemon juice. Reduce the heat and simmer for 8 to 10 minutes, or until the liquid has reduced by half and thickened. Serve warm.

PERSIMMONS WITH POMEGRANATE

The very best side dishes are surprises, like presents that appear on the table to the delight of your dinner guests (and family, too). This brilliant—and brilliantly simple—creation, with its beautiful jewel tones, startlingly fresh flavors, and purely fascinating mix of textures, could not be more of a dinner table star. It's the perfect side for holidays, but take advantage whenever persimmons are in season and whip this one up for even small family gatherings. It's never out of place. ***Serves 4***

2 cups peeled and diced fresh persimmon

2 cups pomegranate seeds

2 tablespoons fresh lime juice

In a large bowl, combine all the ingredients and stir to mix. Refrigerate for 10 minutes or up to 1 hour before serving.

CANDIED YAMS

There are certain dishes that are must-haves for the holidays. Candied yams are essential to the Thanksgiving table, but given how satisfying and easy to make this recipe is, you'll want to make it for other occasions as well. That's because this standard combines the best of a dessert and a side dish. The creamy texture and subtle flavor of the yams would be pleasing all alone, but they are nirvana when coupled with pumpkin-pie spices and the pure fun of a marshmallow topping (a big reason kids go crazy for this dish). **Serves 4 to 6**

3 pounds yams
1 cup (2 sticks) unsalted butter
1½ cups packed brown sugar
½ teaspoon ground cinnamon
¼ teaspoon ground nutmeg
2 cups mini marshmallows

1. Fill a large pot three-quarters full of water and bring to a boil over high heat. Add the yams and cook just until tender, about 15 minutes. Drain and set aside until cool enough to handle.
2. Preheat the oven to 400°F. Butter a 9 x 13-inch baking dish.
3. Peel the yams and cut them into ¼-inch-thick slices. Transfer to a large bowl.
4. In a small saucepan over medium heat, combine the butter, brown sugar, cinnamon, and nutmeg. Cook, stirring, until the butter and sugar have melted. Pour over the yams and stir until the yams are entirely coated.
5. Spread the yams evenly in the prepared baking dish. Bake for 15 minutes. Remove from the oven and cover the top with the marshmallows. Return to the oven and bake until the marshmallows are browned.

CREAMED SPINACH

Properly made creamed spinach requires a bit of a delicate touch. You have to be careful not to cook the greens into oblivion. If they have just a little life and texture left in them, the earthy flavor will blossom against the lavish nature of the cream and butter. A hint of citrus brings some sparkle to the dish, but surprisingly, nutmeg is the key player here. Grate your nutmeg fresh for a fully rounded spice flavor that can't be rivaled by the ground store-bought version. **Serves 4**

2 pounds baby spinach, stems trimmed

1½ cups heavy cream

1 yellow onion, finely chopped

4 tablespoons (½ stick) unsalted butter

¼ cup all-purpose flour

¼ teaspoon freshly grated nutmeg

Kosher salt and freshly ground black pepper

½ teaspoon finely grated lemon zest

1. Fill a large pot with water, salt it heavily, and place over high heat. Fill a large bowl with a mixture of half ice and half cold water. When the water in the pot boils, add the spinach in batches and cook just until the spinach begins to wilt, about 1 minute. Transfer the spinach to the ice water bath to cool and stop the cooking.
2. Once cooled, squeeze all the water out of the spinach and dry it with paper towels.
3. In a small pot over low heat, warm the cream. In a large saucepan over medium heat, melt the butter. Add the onion and cook until soft, about 3 minutes.
4. Whisk the flour into the melted butter to create a roux. Slowly pour in the cream, whisking constantly. Gently simmer until thickened, about 3 minutes. Add the nutmeg, and salt and pepper to taste and stir to combine.
5. Add the spinach and stir, until it is the texture you prefer. When ready to serve, transfer to a serving bowl and sprinkle with the lemon zest.

ON THE SET . . . **WITH BRIDGET**

I'm raising a son, so I'm well aware of just how goofy boys can get when they are not fully occupied. That makes for some amusing moments on the set, because we have two young (and energetic) boys in the cast—brothers Andrew and Tony Terraciano, who play Sean and Jack Reagan on the show. Fortunately, we have another energetic boy on the set named Will Estes. He manages to keep the young brothers occupied between takes. In fact, they have a ritual for the family dinner scene: they all race to see who can be first to the table. I imagine that one day someone's going to overshoot the mark and the props are going to go flying!

POTATOES AU GRATIN

Although there are many ways to prepare potatoes, this preparation represents pota-toes at their comfort-food best. The luscious texture of the perfectly cooked potatoes coated with a lightly spiced cheese sauce makes this an ideal supporting player for heavier main courses, especially beef. This is also a recipe that can be fine-tuned to please your family's palate. Substitute the thyme with your favorite herb, such as oreg-ano, or exchange the cheddar cheese for Gruyère or a similar tangy choice.

Serves 4 to 6

1/2 tablespoon unsalted butter
3 Russet potatoes, peeled and cut into 1/4-inch-thick slices
3 cups half-and-half
1/4 cup all-purpose flour
1 garlic clove, minced
1 shallot, minced

1/2 teaspoon dried thyme
1/2 teaspoon freshly ground white pepper
1/2 teaspoon kosher salt
One 8-ounce bag shredded sharp cheddar cheese

1. Preheat the oven to 350°F. Grease a 2-quart baking dish with the butter.
2. In a large pot, cover the potatoes with cold water. Bring to a boil over medium-high heat. Reduce to a simmer and cook just until the potatoes are tender, 6 to 8 minutes. Drain and set aside.
3. In a large saucepan over medium-high heat, combine the half-and-half and flour and whisk until blended. Add the garlic, shallot, thyme, and white pepper and stir until the sauce boils and thickens, about 7 minutes.
4. Remove the pan from the heat and stir in the salt. Add half the cheese and stir until it melts and is incorporated.
5. Arrange half the potato slices in the bottom of the baking dish. Cover with half the cheese sauce. Top with the remaining potatoes and remaining sauce.
6. Sprinkle the remaining cheese over the top of the dish. Bake for about 20 minutes, or until bubbling. Turn on the broiler and broil until the top is browned, about 1 minute. Serve hot.

STUFFED TOMATOES

*Italian cuisine is famous for making so much out of so few ingredients. We've exploited that in this recipe, where a little basil, some tangy provolone, and bread crumbs combine into a heavenly tomato filling. Once cooked, the tomatoes become wonderfully self-contained, single-serving sides. The tomatoes themselves are more about adding texture because the stuffing flavors dominate. That said, you can put your own stamp on the dish by the tomatoes you use—heirloom varieties, for instance, would create a wonderful varied and pretty look on the table. **Serves 4***

4 large vine-ripened or beefsteak tomatoes
1 cup panko bread crumbs
1 small garlic clove, minced
2 teaspoons minced shallot
$\frac{1}{4}$ cup chopped fresh basil
1 cup grated provolone cheese
$\frac{1}{4}$ cup extra-virgin olive oil

1. Preheat the oven to 400°F.
2. Slice the tomatoes in half horizontally. Using a spoon, scoop out the pulp and seeds, being careful not to puncture the tomato halves.
3. In a large bowl, combine the bread crumbs, garlic, shallot, basil, provolone, and olive oil. Stir to combine, until the bread crumbs are evenly coated with oil.
4. Scoop the filling into the tomato shells, firming and mounding it. Arrange the tomatoes on a small baking sheet, spacing them evenly.
5. Bake for about 30 minutes, or until the tomatoes are soft and the tops are browned. Serve warm.

CORNBREAD

Few side dishes scream "down-home Southern" quite like homemade cornbread. This is a natural partner to barbecue of all types, and anything thick and chunky, like stew or chili. The smell of cornbread coming out of the oven is almost as delightful as the first bite. Almost. But it's hard to top the slightly crunchy, simple goodness of fresh-made cornbread, especially when you smear it with a dose of our own Honey Butter. That combination may just steal a bit of attention away from the main course. **Serves 4 to 6**

CORNBREAD

1 cup yellow cornmeal

³/₄ cup all-purpose flour

1¹/₂ tablespoons sugar

1¹/₂ teaspoons baking powder

¹/₂ teaspoon baking soda

¹/₄ teaspoon salt

2 large eggs, beaten

³/₄ cup buttermilk

³/₄ cup heavy cream

6 tablespoons (³/₄ stick) unsalted butter

HONEY BUTTER

8 tablespoons (1 stick) unsalted butter, softened

1 tablespoon honey

¹/₂ teaspoon ground cinnamon

1. Preheat the oven to 425°F. Butter an 8-inch square baking dish or a 9-inch round cake pan.
2. Make the cornbread: In a large bowl, combine the cornmeal, flour, sugar, baking powder, baking soda, and salt and whisk until completely incorporated.

3. In a small bowl, combine the eggs, buttermilk, cream, and melted butter and whisk to thoroughly mix. Add the liquid mixture to the dry mixture, and stir until entirely combined. Pour the batter into the prepared baking dish or cake pan.
4. Bake the cornbread for 20 minutes, or until the top is golden brown and a toothpick inserted into the center comes out clean. Transfer to a wire rack to cool in the baking dish for 10 minutes before slicing and serving.
5. While the cornbread is cooling, make the honey butter: Combine the butter, honey, and cinnamon in a bowl and beat until smooth and incorporated. Spoon into a ramekin and serve with the cornbread.

BAKED CHEESY RICE

Here's another cold-weather, no-hassle side that will round out any family dinner—from a plain-old weeknight meal to a holiday feast. It's essentially a rice casserole with a dense body and some surprising flavors thanks to the chili powder and chives. The Gruyère cheese adds tang and creaminess. You can dress up the dish with different vegetables in season to make it all your own. **Serve 6**

3 tablespoons unsalted butter
1 yellow onion, chopped
1 red bell pepper, seeded and chopped
One 15-ounce can whole kernel corn
1 large tomato, seeded and chopped
1 teaspoon chopped fresh chives
1 teaspoon kosher salt
½ teaspoon freshly ground black pepper
1 teaspoon chili powder
¾ cup long-grain brown rice, cooked according to package instructions (about 3 cups cooked)
2 cups grated Gruyère cheese

1. Preheat the oven to 425°F.
2. In a large pot over medium heat, melt the butter. Add the onion and bell pepper and cook until softened, 5 to 7 minutes. Add the corn and tomato and cook for 2 minutes.
3. Stir in the chives, salt, black pepper, and chili powder until the vegetables are evenly coated in the spices.
4. Add the cooked rice and half the cheese. Stir until the cheese has completely melted. Transfer to a 2-quart oven-safe casserole dish. Top with the remaining cheese, spreading it in an even layer. Bake for 20 minutes, or until the top begins to brown. Serve hot.

BUTTERMILK BISCUITS

How about some flaky, buttery treasures just like Grandma used to make? This simple recipe lets you whip up buttermilk biscuits that would make a true Southerner proud. They're dense and tangy, but with a buttery sweetness that will either bring back youth-ful memories of sun-filled, smoke-tinged barbecues, or make you yearn to create new ones. These are best eaten with a large dollop of butter or a healthy drizzle of honey. Or combine the two by serving your biscuits with the Honey Butter on page 184. ***Serves 6***

2 cups all-purpose flour
2 teaspoons sugar
2 teaspoons baking powder
$\frac{1}{2}$ teaspoon table salt
10 tablespoons (1 stick plus 2 tablespoons) cold unsalted butter, cubed
1 cup buttermilk

1. Preheat the oven to 375°F.
2. Combine the flour, sugar, baking powder, and salt in a large bowl and whisk thoroughly until completely combined.
3. Add the butter and cut in with a pastry blender or two knives, until the dough has the texture of a coarse meal.
4. Add the buttermilk, about 1 tablespoon at a time, mixing it in with a fork before adding more. When all the buttermilk has been absorbed, use your hands to form the dough into 6 equal balls; do not overwork the dough. Squish and shape the balls into very thick rounds, about 2½ inches in diameter. Place on a baking sheet, spacing them evenly apart.
5. Bake for 25 minutes, or until a toothpick inserted into the center of a biscuit comes out clean. The tops should be light golden brown. Transfer the biscuits to a wire rack to cool for 3 minutes. Serve while still warm.

POPOVERS

Don't you dare buy plain bread when you can easily whip up these fun, cloud-like treats. Unlike denser breads, popovers are filled with air. They look wonderful on the table and go with just any main course you can dream up. The pocket inside can be used to hold butter, Irish Stew (page 160), tomato sauce, honey, whipped cream, or just about any sweet or savory filling, depending on how you want to use the popovers. No matter what goes on (or in!) them, they are simply satisfying without being too filling. **Serves 4 to 6; makes about 10 popovers**

2 tablespoons unsalted butter

2 large eggs, at room temperature, beaten

1 cup half-and-half

1 cup all-purpose flour

½ teaspoon table salt

1 tablespoon grated Parmesan cheese

1. Preheat the oven to 400°F. Liberally grease the cups of a 12-cup muffin pan with the butter. The butter should be thickly applied in each individual cup.
2. In a small bowl, combine the eggs and half-and-half and whisk until the mixture is a uniform color and texture.
3. In a large bowl, sift together the flour and salt. Whisk to ensure they are thoroughly blended, then pour in the egg mixture. Add the Parmesan and whisk until only tiny lumps remain.
4. Preheat the muffin pan in the oven for 4 minutes. Right before you take the pan out of the oven, whisk the batter. Pour the batter into the hot muffin pan, filling each cup a little less than halfway.
5. Bake for 25 minutes without opening the oven door. The popovers should be browned and crisp. Serve warm with butter.

PICKLED DEVILED EGGS

Tired of the same old deviled eggs that you trot out every year for the summer season? Ditch them. There's a new deviled egg in town. Pickling leaves these eggs with an eye-catching fuchsia stain that contrasts with the yellow filling. The filling is a more traditional mustard-based mixture, but the pickled flavor of the egg white gives it a charge that will bring people back to the platter for seconds, thirds, and beyond. You'll likely have a little extra filling—use it as a spread or as a base for a wonderful egg salad. Want to take it over the top? Chop up four slices of crispy cooked bacon and sprinkle them over the eggs just before serving. **Serves 4 to 6**

PICKLING MIXTURE

1 cup distilled white vinegar

1 small red beet, peeled and sliced

1 tablespoon minced yellow onion

1 teaspoon sugar

1 bay leaf

$\frac{1}{2}$ teaspoon kosher salt

PICKLED DEVILED EGGS

6 hard-boiled large eggs, peeled

$\frac{1}{4}$ cup real mayonnaise

1 teaspoon champagne vinegar

1 teaspoon Dijon mustard

$\frac{1}{4}$ teaspoon kosher salt

Freshly ground black pepper

$\frac{1}{2}$ teaspoon smoked paprika

1 teaspoon finely chopped fresh chives

1. Make the pickling mixture: In a large pot over high heat, combine 3 cups water, white vinegar, beet, onion, sugar, bay leaf, and salt and bring to a boil. Reduce the heat to maintain a simmer and cook until the beet is tender, about 20 minutes. Set the pickling mixture aside to cool.

2. Make the pickled deviled eggs: In a large container, combine the cooled pickling mixture with the peeled hard-boiled eggs so that the eggs are submerged in the liquid. Refrigerate for 2 hours.

3. Remove the eggs and discard the pickling liquid. Pat the eggs dry with paper towels. Slice them in half lengthwise and carefully transfer the yolks to a small bowl.

4. Mash the yolks with a fork. Add the mayonnaise, champagne vinegar, mustard, and salt and stir with a fork until smooth. Taste and add salt and pepper as needed.

5. Scoop the yolk mixture into the egg halves with a spoon. Sprinkle the eggs with the paprika and chives. Serve chilled.

GARLIC BREAD

It's bread! No, it's a side dish! No it's something much more than either of those things! Garlic bread is a powerful meal addition that stands just as well on its own. We soaked ours with garlic-infused butter so there's no mistaking what it's all about. Add a sprinkle of paprika and a little dried parsley for color, and you have an ideal accompaniment to lasagna or any other Italian meal. The bread is also absolutely delicious as a snack on the go, or even as part of a tapas menu. Just be sure that whoever you want to kiss eats the bread, too! **Serves 4 to 6**

4 tablespoons (½ stick) unsalted butter

3 large garlic cloves, finely minced

1 small loaf Italian bread

2 teaspoons smoked paprika

1 tablespoon dried parsley

1. Preheat the oven to 350°F.
2. In a small pot over low heat, combine the butter and garlic. Once the butter has melted, let the mixture cook for 10 to 15 minutes.
3. Cut the loaf of bread in half lengthwise and lay the halves, cut-side up, on a baking sheet. Brush or lightly spoon the butter-and-garlic mixture onto the bread, spreading out the garlic so it is distributed evenly. Use all the butter, and make sure the bread is entirely coated.
4. Sprinkle the bread with the paprika, distributing it evenly across the two cut halves. Dust with the parsley, crushing it between your fingers as you sprinkle it over the bread.
5. Toast the bread for 8 to 10 minutes, or until the top surface is crunchy and just beginning to char in some places.
6. Set the bread aside until cool enough to handle, then cut it crosswise into 1-inch-wide strips. Serve while still warm.

ROASTED ROOT VEGETABLES

Nothing makes a winter dinner quite like a big pan of roasted root vegetables coming out of the oven. Roasting brings out a remarkable depth of flavor and the inherent sweetness in these root vegetables. That flavor is boosted when you coat the vegetables lightly in high-quality olive oil and sprinkle them with rosemary. The mix of colors is fun and festive on any holiday table, but don't hesitate to substitute or add other vegetables, such as yellow squash or zucchini, as the season dictates. **Serves 4 to 6**

16 heirloom carrots
2 large parsnips
2 large beets
1 head garlic
2 large sprigs fresh rosemary
¼ cup extra-virgin olive oil
Kosher salt and freshly ground black pepper

1. Preheat the oven to 400°F.
2. Scrub the vegetables clean and trim them. Cut the carrots diagonally into 1-inch slices. Cut the parsnips and beets into 1-inch cubes.
3. Peel and trim the cloves from the head of garlic. Leave the cloves whole.
4. Strip the leaves off the rosemary sprigs, discard the stems, and mince the leaves.
5. In a large bowl, stir together the oil and rosemary. Add the vegetables and toss to coat. Sprinkle with salt and pepper and toss again, ensuring that the vegetables are entirely coated.
6. Spread out the vegetables evenly in a single layer on a rimmed baking sheet. Roast for 50 minutes, or until the edges of the vegetables begin to char and the vegetables are fork-tender. Serve hot.

IRISH SODA BREAD

The Reagan family's dinner table tends toward the traditional, and traditional Irish soda bread was a heavy, dense offering that was just perfect for sopping up soups and stews, or even the juices left over from a steak or roast. The Americanized version often includes raisins and caraway seeds, but we've gone Old Country with our recipe—simple, easy, and filling. This is the sturdiest of breads meant to serve as a stage for strong flavors and spreadable ingredients. This is also a classic to serve on St. Patrick's Day, and is terrific toasted. **Serves 6**

4 cups all-purpose flour
1 teaspoon baking soda
¼ teaspoon table salt
1¾ cups buttermilk

1. Preheat the oven to 450°F. Take a pinch of flour from the measured amount for the bread and lightly flour a baking sheet.
2. In a large bowl, combine the flour, baking soda, and salt. Whisk together until thoroughly incorporated.
3. Make a depression in the middle of the dry mixture and pour in the buttermilk. Using one hand, mix the dough together. Keep mixing until the dough sticks together, without dry, loose areas of flour. Do not overwork the dough.
4. Turn out the dough on a lightly floured work surface. Form it into a round, about 7 inches in diameter. Flip it and score an X in the top from edge to edge, about ⅛ inch deep.
5. Center the dough on the baking sheet and bake for 15 minutes. Reduce the oven temperature to 400°F and bake for 25 minutes more. The top should be golden brown with no areas of char. Tap the bottom—the bread should sound hollow.
6. Transfer to a wire rack and let cool to room temperature, about 1 hour, before slicing and serving.

CRANBERRY SAUCE

A Thanksgiving staple, cranberry sauce should not be confined to one day a year. Much as you may love the canned, jellied variety—and with all due respect to warm and fuzzy childhood memories—this made-from-scratch version is worlds better. The recipe is so basic that you can even prep it the night before. The core of the recipe is super-fresh ingredients, and you can certainly play with the citrus to put a slightly different spin on your own version. Try replacing the orange with Meyer lemon, blood orange, or tangerine for a subtle twist. Then serve it for any special occasion! It is even perfect served with roasted pork loin. **Serves 4**

1 cup fresh orange juice
$\frac{1}{2}$ cup sugar
12 ounces fresh cranberries
Finely grated zest of 1 orange

1. Combine the orange juice and sugar in a medium saucepan. Cook over medium-high heat until the sugar has melted.
2. Add the cranberries and bring to a boil. Watch them closely; boil just until some berries begin to pop. Remove the pot from the heat and stir in the orange zest.
3. Let cool to room temperature and then refrigerate until ready to serve, at least 1 hour and up to overnight.

MASHED POTATOES

*It's the little things that separate great mashed potatoes from okay mashed potatoes— buttermilk instead of milk; a touch of white pepper; a sprinkling of fresh chives. You'll know the difference when you place a big scoop of this on your plate and take your first creamy bite. The flavors are subtle and aren't going to compete with any other dishes on the table, but they are sophisticated enough that you might want to hold off on the gravy or butter. These mashed potatoes hold up just fine on their own. **Serves 4***

2 pounds Russet potatoes, peeled and chopped
1 tablespoon salt
³⁄₄ cup half-and-half
2 tablespoons unsalted butter
¹⁄₄ teaspoon freshly ground white pepper
2 tablespoons buttermilk
Kosher salt and freshly ground black pepper
1 tablespoon chopped fresh chives

1. In a large pot, cover the potatoes with cold water and add the salt. Bring to a boil over medium-high heat and cook until the potatoes are fork-tender, about 15 minutes. Drain the potatoes in a colander.
2. In a medium saucepan over medium-high heat, combine the half-and-half, butter, and white pepper. Heat until the butter has melted, and then whisk in the buttermilk.
3. Mash the potatoes in a large serving bowl with a masher. Add the hot liquid mixture, season with salt and black pepper, and stir thoroughly to combine. Mix in the chives and serve warm.

SWEET BRUSSELS SPROUTS

*If you've never mixed the earthy flavor of Brussels sprouts with some natural sweetness, it's time to take the plunge. You'll be surprised at how well the distinctive flavor of the vegetable works with the teeth-aching sweetness of maple syrup. Throw in just a splash of citrus to moderate the two flavors, and you have a side dish that is sure to become a family favorite. You can make the flavor mix even livelier with a tablespoon of chopped fresh chives or parsley. In any case, blanching the Brussels sprouts ensures that they are a lovely bright green on the table, and pleasantly firm between the teeth. **Serves 4 to 6***

    2 pounds Brussels sprouts, cleaned and trimmed
    2 tablespoons extra-virgin olive oil
    2 tablespoons unsalted butter
    ¼ cup pure maple syrup
    ½ lemon

1. Fill a large bowl with half ice and half cold water. Bring a large pot of at least 6 cups water to boil over high heat. Salt the water heavily and add the Brussels sprouts. Boil the sprouts for 3 minutes, then transfer to the ice water bath. When they are cool, cut the Brussels sprouts in half lengthwise.
2. In a large skillet over medium-high heat, heat the oil. Add the Brussels sprouts and sear, cut-side down, for 3 to 5 minutes. They should just begin to char, but not be burnt; watch them carefully. (Depending on the size of the skillet, you may need to work in batches.)
3. Transfer the Brussels sprouts to a clean bowl. Add the butter and maple syrup to the pan and stir while the butter melts. As soon as the butter has melted, return the Brussels sprouts to the pan and toss to coat.
4. Transfer the Brussels sprouts to a serving dish and drizzle any syrup left in the pan over them. Squeeze the lemon over top and serve warm.

MINTY PEAS

*Mint brightens up any food it touches, and in combination with a little citrus zest, it brings a whole new life to peas. Cooking these "under oil" is a Southern Italian technique that maintains the brightness of both the herb and the peas. We've used frozen peas for this recipe because they are available year-round, but don't hesitate to substitute fresh shucked peas in season. In either case, you'll be whipping up a surprisingly zingy side dish that is chock-full of vitamins and fiber. Make sure you don't overcook the peas, and even the youngsters at the table will give it a fair try. Just don't even think about making this with canned peas. **Serves 4***

1 tablespoon unsalted butter
1 tablespoon extra-virgin olive oil
³⁄₄ cup diced yellow onion
One 10-ounce bag (or box) frozen peas or shucked fresh peas
Kosher salt and freshly ground black pepper
1 tablespoon chopped fresh mint
1¹⁄₂ teaspoons finely grated lemon zest

1. In a large pan over medium heat, melt the butter with the olive oil. Add the onion and cook until soft but not brown.
2. Add the peas and season lightly with salt and pepper. Cook until the peas are just thawed and heated through, about 5 minutes.
3. Remove the pan from the heat and stir in the mint and lemon zest. Serve immediately.

GLAZED CARROTS

This is an accent dish, meant to be served with several other dishes. It offers a bright splash of jubilant color and injects a lovely understated sweetness to the meal. Although the classic version of glazed carrots uses brown sugar, we feel that's just a bit heavy-handed. We like the more natural sweetness of honey or maple syrup—you can even substitute agave if you prefer. A splash of lemon juice cuts all the sweetness in the dish, as does a tiny dose of chili powder. The ingredients and flavors mesh perfectly.

Serves 4 to 6

> 1 teaspoon kosher salt
>
> 1 pound carrots, peeled and sliced diagonally
>
> 2 tablespoons unsalted butter
>
> 2 tablespoons honey (or substitute maple syrup)
>
> 1 tablespoon fresh lemon juice
>
> 1/4 teaspoon freshly ground white pepper
>
> Dash of chili powder
>
> 1 teaspoon finely grated lemon zest
>
> 2 tablespoons chopped fresh chives

1. In a large saucepan, bring 5 cups of water to a boil over high heat. Add the salt and carrots and cook until tender, about 5 minutes. Drain the carrots in a colander.

2. Remove the pan from the heat and add the butter, honey, lemon juice, white pepper, and chili powder. Stir until the butter melts, then add the carrots and return the pan to medium heat.

3. Cook for about 5 minutes, tossing the carrots occasionally, until the glaze coats the carrots. Sprinkle with the lemon zest and toss one last time. Transfer to a serving bowl and sprinkle with the chives just before serving.

GREEN BEANS AMANDINE

Anytime you're crowding a family dinner table with heavy, rich dishes, a simple, tasty vegetable recipe like this can be a welcome respite. A tiny splash of butter is all the decadence this dish needs to soar. Toasted almonds add sweetness that contrasts the simple garden-fresh taste of the beans. The crunch of one heightens the crunch of the other. You can substitute standard green beans for the haricots verts, but we recommend making the effort to find the French variety—they are more elegant both to eat and to look at. **Serves 4**

> 1 pound haricots verts (or substitute regular green beans), trimmed
> 1/4 cup slivered almonds
> 2 tablespoons unsalted butter
> 2 tablespoons extra-virgin olive oil
> 1 large shallot, minced
> Kosher salt and freshly ground black pepper
> Finely grated zest and juice of 1/2 lemon

1. Fill a large pot with heavily salted water and bring to a boil. Fill a large bowl with a mixture of half ice and half cold water. Blanch the haricots verts in the boiling water for 1½ minutes. Drain and plunge into the ice water bath to cool and stop the cooking.
2. While the haricots verts cool, toast the almonds in a large pan over high heat, turning them constantly. Be careful not to burn the almonds. Set aside.
3. Reduce the heat to medium-high. Add the butter and olive oil to the pan. When the butter has melted, add the shallot. Season with salt and pepper and cook just until the shallots is soft and starting to color.
4. Add the cooled haricots verts to the pan and toss to coat. Add the lemon zest and juice and toss again. Cook until the haricots verts are heated through, about 2 minutes.
5. Transfer to a serving dish and add the almonds. Toss, taste, and add salt and pepper as needed. Serve warm.

DESSERTS

PECAN PIE

This dessert is a marriage of the sweetness of nuts to a timeless custard that was first used in the Southern chess pie. The pie is meant to be so sweet that your teeth ache, which means a small piece suffices—especially when served with a cup of piping hot coffee. We've kept with tradition and infused our pie filling with loving amounts of corn syrup and brown sugar. It is exactly what it's supposed to be—the perfect finish to a big meal. It's also unbelievably easy and quick to make. **Serves 4 to 6**

One 1/4-ounce envelope unflavored
   gelatin
One 6-ounce bag pecan halves
3 large eggs
1/2 cup packed dark brown sugar
1 cup dark corn syrup

1/2 teaspoon salt
2 teaspoons pure vanilla extract
4 tablespoons (1/2 stick) unsalted
   butter, melted and cooled to
   room temperature
One 9-inch unbaked pie shell

1. Preheat the oven to 375°F.
2. In a small bowl, pour the gelatin into 1/3 cup hot water and stir until dissolved. Set aside to cool. Chop 1 cup of the pecans into coarse pieces; reserve the remaining pecan halves.
3. In a large bowl, beat the eggs well. Add the brown sugar, corn syrup, salt, and vanilla and stir until thoroughly mixed.
4. Add the melted butter and stir until the butter is completely incorporated. Add the cooled gelatin and stir until combined, scraping down the sides of the bowl as you stir.
5. Add the chopped pecans and stir until evenly distributed throughout the mixture. Add the whole pecans and stir just until mixed in, being careful not to break them.
6. Pour the mixture into the pie shell. Bake for 45 minutes, or until the edges of the pie shell are light golden brown (not dark brown) and the center is firm. Transfer the pie to a wire rack and cool before serving.

STRAWBERRY SHORTCAKES

*The heart of any strawberry shortcake recipe is freshness. As far as we're concerned, strawberry shortcake using frozen strawberries or store-bought sponge cakes is a weak pretender to the throne. Go the extra mile and find fresh strawberries, and make sure they are truly ripe (you want each one to burst with flavor when eaten). Then spend a little time and effort making the shortcakes and whipped cream from scratch (our shortcakes are airy and delicate, but you can substitute the Buttermilk Biscuits on page 187 if you prefer a denser shortcake). The difference will be appreciated by everyone around your table! **Serves 6***

STRAWBERRIES

    2 quarts strawberries, cleaned, hulled, and chopped

    Juice of 1 large lemon

    Juice of 1 large orange

    1 1/2 tablespoons sugar

    Fresh mint leaves, for garnish

SHORTCAKES

    2 cups all-purpose flour

    2 1/2 teaspoons baking powder

    1/2 teaspoon salt

    3 tablespoons sugar

    8 tablespoons (1 stick) cold unsalted butter, cut into small cubes

    3/4 cup whole milk

WHIPPED CREAM

    2 cups heavy cream

    1 1/2 tablespoons sugar

    1/2 teaspoon pure vanilla extract

1. Prepare the strawberries: Put the strawberries in a large glass bowl. Top with the fruit juices and sprinkle the sugar on top. Gently mix until the strawberries are completely coated. Cover and refrigerate for at least 2 hours or up to 6 hours.
2. Make the shortcakes: Preheat the oven to 400°F.
3. In a medium bowl, whisk together the flour, baking powder, and salt. Sift this mixture with the sugar into a large bowl.
4. Add the cold butter and cut it in with a pastry blender or two knives, until the mixture is composed of balls the size of BBs. Add the milk, 1 tablespoon at a time, mixing it in with a fork. Continue mixing until all the milk is added, but try not to overwork the dough.
5. Form the dough into 6 equal balls and place them on a nonstick baking sheet, spacing them evenly apart. Squish and form the balls into "pucks" 2½ to 3 inches in diameter. Bake the shortcakes for about 20 minutes, or until light golden brown on top. Transfer to a wire rack to cool.
6. Make the whipped cream: In the bowl of a stand mixer or in a large bowl using a hand mixer, combine the cream, sugar, and vanilla and beat on medium speed until stiff peaks form.
7. Assemble the shortcakes: Cut the top third off each shortcake and place each bottom in the center of a dessert plate. Evenly divide the juice and strawberries among the shortcake bottoms, covering them but reserving a small amount of the juice.
8. Cover the strawberries with a healthy serving of whipped cream, put the top of the shortcake on the whipped cream, and drizzle each with the remaining fruit juice. Top with a dollop of whipped cream, garnish with mint leaves, and serve.

ANDREW AND TONY'S SIMPLE CHOCOLATE CHIP COOKIES

Andrew and Tony Terraciano play brothers Sean and Jack Reagan on the show, and are the youngest members of the Blue Bloods *cast. Both have a sweet tooth, and their mother says they like to make these super-chewy, moist and deep chocolaty cookies on a regular basis.* **Makes about 24 cookies**

2 cups all-purpose flour

½ teaspoon baking soda

½ teaspoon sea salt

½ tablespoon ground cinnamon

¾ cup (1½ sticks) butter, melted until lightly browned

1 cup packed brown sugar

½ cup granulated sugar

1 large egg

1 large egg yolk

2 teaspoons pure vanilla extract

One 12-ounce bag dark chocolate chips

1. Preheat the oven to 350°F. Line two large baking sheets with parchment paper.
2. In a small bowl, sift together the flour, baking soda, and salt.
3. Transfer the butter to the bowl, of a stand mixer, or a large bowl if you're using a hand beater. Add the sugars and beat until combined. Add the egg, egg yolk, and vanilla and beat until incorporated.
4. Slowly add the flour in small batches, beating until incorporated. When the dough is a uniform texture, fold in the chocolate chips with a large wooden spoon.
5. Scoop rounded tablespoons of the cookie dough onto the prepared baking sheets, leaving about 2 inches between cookies. Bake for 10 to 12 minutes, until the edges just begin to brown and the middles are soft. Remove and let cool on the baking sheet. Serve when cool enough to handle.

CLASSIC NEW YORK–STYLE CHEESECAKE

There are two types of cheesecake in the world: coarse-textured Italian cheesecake made with ricotta cheese, and the smooth and creamy New York–style cheesecake made with cream cheese and sour cream. If you're a New York Irish family, you go for the New York–style. Ours has a blue topping in honor of the NYPD and their uniforms—see the box on page 216 for the recipe. This cheesecake is silky smooth with a melt-on-your-tongue texture. We make our crust with walnuts in addition to the classic graham crackers, which give it a crunchier, slightly more interesting taste and texture. The secret to a crack-free New York–style cheesecake is a water bath underneath the cake while baking. Bake it carefully, and this super-creamy dessert will look as beautiful as it tastes. ***Serves 6 to 8***

CRUST

- 2 cups crushed graham crackers
- 1 cup finely diced walnuts
- ⅓ cup confectioners' sugar
- 8 tablespoons (1 stick) unsalted butter, melted

CHEESECAKE

- Four 8-ounce packages cream cheese, softened
- 5 large eggs
- 1 cup granulated sugar
- 2 teaspoons pure vanilla extract
- 3 cups sour cream

1. Preheat the oven to 350°F.
2. Make the crust: In a medium bowl, combine the graham crackers, walnuts, and confectioners' sugar and stir until well mixed. Slowly pour in the melted butter, stirring with a fork until the dry ingredients are thoroughly coated and an even texture.
3. Transfer the mixture to a 10-inch springform pan. Using the back of a large spoon, firm the mixture into place along the bottom and halfway up the sides of the pan. Press to ensure the crust is an even thickness all over. Refrigerate the crust.
4. Make the filling: In the bowl of a stand mixer, or in a large bowl if using a hand mixer, combine the softened cream cheese, eggs, granulated sugar, and vanilla. Beat on low until the filling is smooth.

5. Assemble the cheesecake: Pour the filling into the chilled crust. Wrap the bottom of the springform pan in aluminum foil to protect against leaks. Sit the pan in a high-sided baking sheet or large roasting pan and add warm water to come about 1 inch up the sides of the springform pan. Bake the cheesecake for 50 minutes.

6. Remove the cheesecake from the oven, dollop the sour cream on top, and spread it in an even layer. Return the cheesecake to the oven and bake for 10 minutes. Remove from the oven and let cool to room temperature.

7. Cover the top of the pan with plastic wrap and refrigerate. When the cheesecake is chilled, carefully run a thin knife around the edges before removing the cake from the springform pan. Use a hot knife to cut slices, cleaning the knife between each cut.

BLUE **BLOODS** KITCHEN **TIP**

Macerating fruit is a wonderful way to make toppings for pastry, ice cream, cakes, and other desserts. The process uses sugar and an acid (normally citrus, but sometimes vinegar) to break down fruit and draw out flavors and juices. You can alter the flavor of the fruit slightly through your choice of citrus. The fruit should be refrigerated for hours if possible, to make the topping as syrupy as possible. You can also use a shortcut if time is limited. Simmer the same ingredients in a small saucepot for about five minutes, or until the fruit begins to break down. Let it cool before using, or serve it hot, if you prefer.

NYPD BLUE CHEESECAKE TOPPING
   1 pint fresh blueberries (or substitute frozen out of season)
   Finely grated zest and juice of 1 lemon
   3 tablespoons sugar

Combine the ingredients in a glass bowl and stir until the fruit is completely coated. Cover and refrigerate for at least 3 hours, or until ready to use. Carefully spread the blueberry topping evenly across the top of the cake, or give your dinner guests more control over their dessert by serving the cheesecake with the topping on the side.

PUMPKIN PIE TWO WAYS

It's the rare cook who dares to put together a Thanksgiving meal without pumpkin pie at the end. But people often forget how wonderful this dessert can be at any time of the year. Especially when you have the option of a traditional version or a cloud-light style that eats almost like a soufflé. Pick the one that best suits your crowd (or do what we do, and always make both). Either way, you must use pure pumpkin puree rather than canned pumpkin pie mix—the puree lends a sturdier, more authentic flavor to either recipe.

TRADITIONAL PUMPKIN PIE

Serves 6 to 8

One 15-ounce can 100 percent pure pumpkin puree (not pumpkin pie mix)
1 teaspoon ground cinnamon
¼ teaspoon ground ginger
¼ teaspoon ground nutmeg
¼ teaspoon ground cloves
½ teaspoon sea salt
2 large eggs, beaten
One 14-ounce can sweetened condensed milk
One frozen 9-inch deep-dish pie shell

1. Preheat the oven to 425°F.
2. In a large bowl, combine the pumpkin puree, cinnamon, ginger, nutmeg, cloves, and salt and stir until completely incorporated. Add the eggs and condensed milk and stir until the filling is a uniform color and texture. Pour the filling into the pie shell.
3. Bake the pie for 15 minutes, then reduce the oven temperature to 350°F and bake for 40 minutes more, or until the edges of the filling are set and the center still jiggles slightly.
4. Cool the pie on a wire rack to room temperature. Serve, or refrigerate to chill before serving.

"CHEESCAKEY" PUMPKIN PIE

Serves 6 to 8

4 ounces cream cheese, softened
½ cup granulated sugar
¼ cup packed dark brown sugar
One 15-ounce can 100 percent pure pumpkin puree (not pumpkin pie mix)
1 teaspoon ground cinnamon
½ teaspoon ground ginger
¼ teaspoon ground nutmeg
¼ teaspoon kosher salt
3 large eggs, beaten
½ cup heavy cream
1 teaspoon pure vanilla extract
One frozen 9-inch deep-dish pie shell

1. Preheat the oven to 350°F.
2. In the bowl of a stand mixer, or in a large bowl using a hand mixer, combine the cream cheese and granulated and brown sugars. With the mixer on medium-low speed, beat until creamy and uniform.
3. Add the pumpkin puree, cinnamon, ginger, nutmeg, and salt and beat until completely incorporated, scraping down the sides of the bowl, as necessary, with a spatula.
4. Add the eggs, heavy cream, and vanilla and beat until the filling is smooth and has a uniform color and texture. Pour the filling into the pie shell.
5. Place the pie plate on a small baking sheet with a high rim. Carefully fill the baking sheet with warm water. Place the baking sheet in the oven.
6. Bake the pie for 45 minutes, or until the edges are set and puffed up and the center still jiggles slightly. Cool on a wire rack to room temperature. Once at room temperature, refrigerate the pie for several hours, or until completely chilled, before serving.

BEHIND THE SCENES . . . **WITH WENDY**

Donnie Wahlberg is such a natural as Detective Danny Reagan, and such a key part of the *Blue Bloods* family, that it's incredible to think he almost wasn't cast for the part. Most of the cast had already been chosen for the show and the producers were prepping to shoot the pilot. They had seen Donnie's reel and thought highly of him. He had read the script and loved the character, but they wouldn't have a chance to meet because the producers and director were in Toronto. As luck would have it, at the eleventh hour they learned that Donnie was in Toronto on music business! They tracked him down, he met with the producers and director, and it was a perfect fit from the start. The rest is wonderful *Blue Bloods* history.

BERRY COBBLER

Rumor has it that berries were invented so that bakers could make cobbler. It's no wonder that many countries have a version of this heartwarming and tongue-pleasing dessert. Our version doesn't enclose the fruit in pastry, but instead, tops the filling with a fabulously flaky crust. That light and dry topping is the perfect counterpoint to the thick juice and hot, soft berries beneath. The fresh-picked sweetness and sizzling fruit syrup bubbling up through delicate pastry top is almost enough to make you wish you hadn't bothered with dinner. **Serves 6**

FILLING

½ cup granulated sugar

2 tablespoons cornstarch

Two 12-ounce packages frozen mixed berries (or substitute 6 cups fresh in season)

½ teaspoon finely grated lemon zest

TOPPING

1⅓ cups all-purpose flour

¼ cup granulated sugar

1½ teaspoons baking powder

½ teaspoon salt

5 tablespoons cold unsalted butter, cubed

½ cup heavy cream

1 large egg

2 tablespoons Sugar in the Raw

1. Preheat the oven to 400°F.
2. Make the filling: In a large bowl, combine the granulated sugar and cornstarch and whisk until thoroughly mixed. Add the berries and lemon zest and stir until the berries are completely coated. Pour the mixture into a 2-quart oven–safe casserole dish.
3. Make the topping: Sift the flour, granulated sugar, baking powder, and salt into a large bowl. Add the butter and cut it into the dry ingredients with a pastry blender or two knives, until the mixture has the texture of coarse meal.

4. Add the cream and mix it in with a fork until a dough forms. Dust a work surface and your hands with flour. Gather the dough into a ball.

5. Knead the dough gently for about 1 minute, than flatten the ball. Lightly roll out the dough, reshaping it into a rectangle or oval that matches the top of your casserole dish.

6. Lay the dough on top of the berries in the dish. In a small bowl, whisk the egg with 1 tablespoon of water until milky. Brush the dough with the egg wash and sprinkle with the Sugar in the Raw.

7. Bake the cobbler for 35 minutes, or until the top is golden brown. Let rest for at least 10 minutes before serving.

CARROT CAKE

It might seem odd to make a dessert with a vegetable, but carrots are a natural choice for cake. The orange veggie has some of the highest natural sugar content among garden produce, and it gifts any baked good with a moist texture courtesy of its wonderful water-retaining properties. We've topped this nutty cake with tried-and-true cream cheese frosting. Some people like their carrot cake iced with a slab of frosting, but the amount this recipe makes provides just a light layer. Double the frosting if you prefer your icing thick. **Serves 4 to 6**

CAKE

1 cup packed brown sugar

1 cup granulated sugar

1 teaspoon salt

2 teaspoons ground cinnamon

$^1/_2$ teaspoon ground ginger

2 cups safflower oil

4 large eggs, beaten

2 cups pastry flour

2 teaspoons baking powder

1$^1/_2$ teaspoons baking soda

2 cups grated carrots

Two 8-ounce cans crushed pineapple, undrained

$^1/_2$ cup finely chopped walnuts

FROSTING

8 tablespoons cream cheese, at room temperature

6 tablespoons ($^3/_4$ stick) unsalted butter, at room temperature

1$^1/_2$ teaspoons pure vanilla extract

$^1/_2$ cup confectioners' sugar

Finely grated zest of 1 large orange

1. Make the cake: Preheat the oven to 350°F. Grease a 9 x 13-inch baking pan.

2. In a large bowl, combine the brown and granulated sugars, salt, cinnamon, and ginger and stir with a fork to blend. Add the oil and eggs and mix with a fork until incorporated.

3. Add the flour, baking powder, and baking soda and stir until completely combined. Add the carrots, pineapple, and walnuts and mix until the batter is a uniform texture.

4. Pour the batter into the prepared baking pan and bake for 50 minutes, or until a toothpick inserted into the center of the cake comes out clean. Remove from the oven and let cool to room temperature.

5. Make the frosting: In the bowl of a stand mixer, or in a large bowl if using a hand mixer, combine the cream cheese, butter, vanilla, and confectioners' sugar. Beat on low until smooth and fluffy.

6. Spread the frosting on the cake with a knife or spatula. Sprinkle the orange zest evenly across the top. Slice and serve.

NIKKI'S RED **VELVET** CUPCAKES **WITH** ERMINE **FROSTING**

The best sweet treats please the eye as well as the tongue, and that's where this one really shines. We use a beet to color the batter, just as they did in Colonial times when sugar was not only a rarity, but was also often impossible to get. Beets provided the sweetness, but they also held in moisture and tinted anything they touched an alluring magenta. The original Red Velvet dessert was a cake, and you can easily convert this recipe back to its pure roots by baking the batter in cake pans. The wonderful ermine frosting—with a depth of flavor far beyond any other frosting—remains the same either way. **Makes 20 to 24 cupcakes**

CUPCAKES

1 small red beet

2 cups cake flour

2 tablespoons unsweetened
  cocoa powder

1³/₄ teaspoons baking powder

¹/₂ teaspoon baking soda

³/₄ teaspoon salt

¹/₃ cup canola oil

10 tablespoons (1 stick plus
  2 tablespoons) unsalted butter

1³/₄ cups sugar

2 teaspoons pure vanilla extract

1 teaspoon almond extract

¹/₂ teaspoon finely grated orange zest

4 large eggs

³/₄ cup buttermilk

Juice of 1 lemon

ERMINE FROSTING

6 tablespoons all-purpose flour

2 cups whole milk

2 teaspoons pure vanilla extract

Pinch of salt

1¹/₂ cups (3 sticks) unsalted butter,
  softened

1¹/₄ cups sugar

1. Make the cupcakes: Preheat the oven to 350°F. Line a muffin pan with paper liners.
2. Scrub the beet thoroughly and let dry. Wrap the beet tightly in aluminum foil and roast for about 1 hour, or until a knife inserted into the beet goes in easily to the center. Remove from the oven, peel off the foil, and let cool.

3. In a medium bowl, sift together the flour, cocoa, baking powder, baking soda, and salt. Set aside.
4. Chop the cooled beet and combine with the oil in a food processor. Pulse until smooth.
5. In the bowl of a stand mixer, or in a large bowl using a hand mixer, beat the butter and sugar on low until creamy, about 5 minutes. Add the vanilla, almond extract, and orange zest and beat until incorporated.
6. Add the eggs, one at a time, beating until each is fully incorporated before adding the next. Add the buttermilk and beat until smooth. Add the beet mixture and beat until incorporated.
7. Slowly add the dry mixture, a little at a time, and beat until the batter is smooth and a uniform color. Add the lemon juice and beat until incorporated into the batter.
8. Spoon the batter into the lined muffin cups, filling each to the top. Be careful not to drip on the edges of the muffin pan. Bake for 17 to 20 minutes, or until a toothpick inserted into the center of a cupcake comes out clean.
9. Remove from the oven and allow the cupcakes to cool in the pan until cool enough to handle. Transfer the cupcakes to a wire rack to finish cooling.
10. While the cupcakes are cooling, make the ermine frosting: In a saucepan over medium-low heat, combine the flour and milk and cook, whisking constantly, until the mixture has the texture of syrup.
11. Remove the pan from the heat and whisk in the vanilla and salt. Transfer to a small bowl and cover with plastic wrap, pressing it directly on the surface of the mixture to prevent a skin from forming. Refrigerate for 15 to 20 minutes.
12. In the bowl of a stand mixer, or in a large bowl if using a hand mixer, combine the butter and sugar. Beat on medium speed until light and fluffy, about 4 minutes. Add the flour, a little at a time, with the mixer running on low. Increase the speed to medium and beat the frosting until it has a smooth, creamy, uniform texture. This may take a long time—don't be discouraged if the frosting breaks at first.
13. Fill a pastry bag with the frosting (or use a resealable sandwich bag with a corner snipped off) and swirl the frosting on top of each cupcake.

ROULADE LÉONTINE

It takes an awfully incredible dessert to pull off a grand name like Roulade Léontine, but this special occasion jaw-dropper manages to pull it off. Irish families much like the Reagans regularly roll out this perfect dessert for family dinners celebrating rare occasions such as graduations and job promotions. It looks beautiful on the table, and tastes like cocoa-flavored clouds. We add a bit of orange liqueur to the filling, but you can certainly leave it out if that's not to your taste—the dessert will still be the high point of the meal. **Serves 6 to 8**

CAKE

6 ounces bittersweet chocolate, chopped (preferably Ghirardelli)

3 tablespoons strong, dark coffee

6 large eggs, at room temperature, separated

⅔ cup granulated sugar

¼ teaspoon salt

1 tablespoon unsweetened cocoa powder

FILLING

1 cup heavy cream

3 tablespoons confectioners' sugar, sifted

1 teaspoon Cointreau (or substitute Grand Marnier)

½ teaspoon finely grated orange zest

FINISHING

Unsweetened cocoa powder, sifted

Confectioner's sugar, sifted

1. Make the cake: Preheat the oven to 350°F. Grease a 15 x 10–inch baking pan (or similar) and line the bottom of the pan with parchment paper along its length, leaving 1 to 2 inches of overlap on each end.
2. Combine the chocolate and coffee in the top of a double boiler and melt the chocolate over simmering water. Remove from the heat and set aside to cool slightly.

3. In a large bowl, combine the egg yolks and ⅓ cup of the granulated sugar. Use a hand mixer and beat on medium speed until pale and the thickness of pudding, about 3 minutes. Fold in the melted chocolate and stir until incorporated.

4. Clean the beaters thoroughly. In a medium bowl, use a hand mixer to beat the egg whites and salt until they hold soft peaks. Slowly add the remaining ⅓ cup granulated sugar and beat until stiff peaks form.

5. Using a spatula, carefully fold the egg whites into the chocolate mix, about one-third at a time, and stir with the spatula until completely incorporated. Spread the batter evenly across the prepared baking pan.

6. Bake the cake until the top is puffy and dry, 13 to 15 minutes. Transfer the pan to a wire rack and cover the cake with two layers of clean, light, cotton dish towels that have been dampened slightly. (Or use paper towels.) Let rest for 5 minutes, then remove the towels and allow the cake to cool completely.

7. Sift the cocoa over the top of the cooled cake. Lay layers of wax paper over top, so that the top of the cake is covered. Set another large baking sheet on top of the cake, top-side down, and carefully invert the cake onto the baking sheet.

8. Slowly and carefully peel off the parchment paper to expose the bottom of the cake. Some small sections will come off with the paper, but that is natural.

9. Make the filling: In a large bowl, combine the cream, confectioners' sugar, and Cointreau. Using a hand mixer, beat on medium until the mixture holds stiff peaks. Gently fold in the orange zest, mixing it thoroughly to disperse it throughout the filling.

10. Using a flat pastry knife or hard spatula, spread the filling in an even layer over the cake. Using the wax paper as a handle, gently roll the cake up from one short end. The cake may crack on the outside, but don't worry, it will stay intact. Roll it up entirely.

11. To finish, dust the roulade with sifted cocoa powder, and then a layer of sifted confectioners' sugar. Serve immediately, or cover with plastic wrap and chill until serving time.

SHORTBREAD AND IRISH COFFEE

Irish coffee isn't really Irish at all. It was just named that for the type of whiskey used in the perky beverage. Of course, shortbread isn't a shamrock treat either. But that doesn't stop this from being a purely delightful meal-ending combination. Both are as easy to make as they are to consume, and shortbread will keep for weeks in an airtight container. Even if the meal has been heavy and large, you'll find the shortbread just sweet enough to finish the meal off with a small exclamation point, and the double warmth of the whiskey and coffee are the perfect way to cap a wonderful evening. **Serves 4 to 6**

SHORTBREAD
2 cups all-purpose flour

1 teaspoon salt

1 cup (2 sticks) unsalted butter, softened

1/2 cup sugar

IRISH COFFEE
1 cup heavy cream

4 to 6 teaspoons sugar (1 teaspoon per glass)

8 cups fresh-brewed dark roast coffee

4 to 6 shots Irish whiskey (1 shot per glass)

1. Make the shortbread: Preheat the oven to 350°F. Grease a 10-inch springform pan.
2. In a small bowl, sift together the flour and salt, and whisk thoroughly after sifting.
3. In the bowl of a stand mixer, or in a large bowl if using a hand mixer, beat the butter on medium speed until fluffy, about 2 minutes. Add the sugar and beat until combined and fluffy, about 2 minutes, scraping down the sides of the bowl as necessary during beating.
4. Add the flour mixture to the butter, one-third at a time. Beat the first two additions just until incorporated. Beat the final addition until the mixture is uniform pebble-size pieces and holds together when squeezed.
5. Press the shortbread into the prepared springform pan in a uniform layer. Score

the top deeply into single-serving wedges. Prick the top all over with the tines of a fork, creating a uniform pattern.

6. Bake until the shortbread is firm and the top is light golden brown, about 50 minutes. Transfer to a wire rack to cool. When completely cool, cut into wedges.

7. Make the Irish coffee: In a chilled medium glass bowl, whip the cream until it holds stiff peaks.

8. Put the sugar in the bottom of warmed, heatproof stem glasses or mugs.

9. Pour the coffee into the glasses and add the whiskey. Carefully dollop the whipped cream on top of the coffee and serve with the shortbread.

DRUGSTORE CHOCOLATE **CAKE**

If you were alive when somebody like Frank Reagan was a child, you might have enjoyed the wonder of the drugstore lunch counter. These small diners-within-a-store were fixtures throughout America. Families could do a bit of shopping and then sit down and treat themselves to a special lunch. Along with the tuna melt and egg cream, patrons would almost always find a simple layer cake in chocolate or vanilla. We've gone with a chocolate frosting covering airy coffee-flavored layers for our spin on the classic drugstore cake. This is the ideal way to get your chocolate-and-sugar fix for the month, and transport yourself back to a simpler time and place. ***Serves 6 to 8***

CAKE

2 cups cake flour

1$\frac{1}{2}$ teaspoons baking powder

$\frac{1}{2}$ teaspoon baking soda

$\frac{1}{2}$ teaspoon salt

$\frac{3}{4}$ cup unsweetened cocoa powder

1 $\frac{3}{4}$ cups granulated sugar

8 tablespoons (1 stick) unsalted butter, cubed and softened

$\frac{1}{3}$ cup canola oil

1 teaspoon pure vanilla extract

1 cup heavy cream

$\frac{1}{2}$ cup brewed espresso, cooled

1 teaspoon coffee-flavored liqueur

4 large eggs

FROSTING

3 cups confectioners' sugar

1 cup unsweetened cocoa powder

1$\frac{1}{2}$ cups (3 sticks) unsalted butter, softened

1 tablespoon pure vanilla extract

$\frac{3}{4}$ cup heavy cream

1. Make the cake: Preheat the oven to 350°F. Grease two 9-inch round cake pans and dust with flour.

2. In the bowl of a stand mixer or in a large bowl if using a hand mixer, sift together the flour, baking powder, baking soda, salt, and cocoa. Add the granulated sugar and stir thoroughly to completely combine.

3. Add the butter and beat on low speed for about 2 minutes, or until it is completely cut into the dry mix. With the mixer running, pour in the oil and beat until the mixture has the consistency of sand.

4. In a small bowl, combine the vanilla, cream, espresso, and coffee liqueur and whisk to thoroughly mix. Add this mixture to the mixer bowl and beat on low speed for about 2 minutes, or until completely incorporated, scraping down the sides of the bowl as necessary.

5. Add the eggs, one at a time. Beat on medium, until each egg is completely incorporated before adding the next.

6. Pour the batter into the prepared pans and bake for 30 minutes, or until a toothpick inserted into the center comes out clean. Cool the cakes in the pans on a wire rack. When they are completely cool, carefully remove them from the pans.

7. Make the frosting: In a large bowl, sift together the confectioners' sugar and cocoa. Set aside.

8. In the bowl of a stand mixer, or in a large bowl with hand mixer, combine the butter and vanilla and beat on low for 1 minute, or until creamed. Slowly add a quarter of the dry mixture. Add 2 tablespoons of the heavy cream while beating on low. Repeat until all the dry mixture and cream have been added and the frosting is a uniform texture.

9. Assemble the cake: Place one cake layer on a large flat plate or cake stand. Using a flat pastry knife, spread the frosting across the top in a thick layer. Sit the second cake layer on top of the first, and spread frosting evenly across the top and down the sides. Clean the knife and smooth the frosting. Slice the cake with a hot knife when you're ready to serve.

BLACK & WHITE COOKIES

If the Reagan family were a real-life New York clan, every one of them would have happy memories of black-&-white cookies bought fresh at a local bakery. Also known as "half-and-halfs," these light-as-air treats are as much a part of New York City as the Empire State Building. A single cookie answers cravings for two sweets, with one half of the top coated in vanilla icing, and the other half in chocolate. **Serves 4; makes 4 to 6 cookies**

COOKIES

1¼ cups cake flour

½ teaspoon baking soda

½ teaspoon salt

¼ cup buttermilk

1 teaspoon pure vanilla extract

6 tablespoons (¾ stick) unsalted butter, softened

½ cup granulated sugar

1 large egg

ICING

1¾ cups confectioners' sugar

2 tablespoons light corn syrup

2 teaspoons fresh lemon juice

½ teaspoon pure vanilla extract

2 tablespoons unsweetened cocoa powder, plus more as needed to darken color

1. Make the cookies: Preheat the oven to 350°F. Grease a large baking sheet.
2. In a small bowl, whisk together the flour, baking soda, and salt. In a separate bowl, combine the buttermilk and vanilla and stir to mix.
3. In the bowl of a stand mixer, or in a large mixing bowl if using a hand mixer, combine the butter and granulated sugar and beat on low until fluffy, about 5 minutes. Add the egg and beat until incorporated.
4. Add a quarter of the flour mixture and beat until incorporated. Add a third of the

buttermilk mixture and beat until incorporated. Alternate adding the two until you've incorporated all the ingredients. The batter should be smooth and sticky.

5. Scoop ½ cup of batter onto the baking sheet. Form into a 3½-inch circle and, using a buttered knife, smooth the top flat. Repeat with the remaining batter, leaving at least 2 inches between cookies.

6. Bake the cookies for about 15 minutes, or until the tops are just golden brown and the center is springy. Let cool on the baking sheet for 1 to 2 minutes, then transfer to a wire rack to cool completely.

7. Make the icing: Combine the confectioners' sugar, 1 tablespoon of the corn syrup, the lemon juice, and vanilla in a small bowl. Whisk thoroughly until there are no lumps and the icing is a uniform white color.

8. When the cookies have cooled to room temperature, set the cookies on a long sheet of wax paper. Fold and crease a separate square of wax paper to serve as a straight edge. Hold the creased edge of the paper across the center of a cookie and brush or spread the while icing with a knife across the exposed half of the cookie. Repeat with the rest of the cookies. Allow them to dry until the icing is tacky. Apply a second layer of white icing as needed (the icing may absorb into the cookie).

9. Add the cocoa and remaining 1 tablespoon corn syrup to the remaining icing and stir until completely incorporated. The icing should be almost black. Ice the other half of the cookies, using the same method as with the white icing. Let the icing harden for at least 30 minutes before serving.

APPLE PIE

As purely American as apple pie seems, it can trace its roots back to merry old England and a centuries-old tradition of tarts, pies, and pie-like "puddings." Americans in Betsy Ross's time turned to apples because they carried their own natural sweetness at a time when sugar was a precious, and expensive, commodity. But the apples, more specifically the vast number of varieties, also provide a way to put your own signature on the pie. We've included a mix of tart and sweet apples, but choose yours based on which way you lean. No matter what apples you use, we recommend garnishing each slice of pie with the tried-and-true scoop of vanilla ice cream, or a thick slice of cheddar cheese.

Serves 4 to 6

2 frozen pie crust sheets, defrosted

$^3/_4$ cup sugar

3 tablespoons all-purpose flour

$^1/_8$ teaspoon salt

$^1/_2$ teaspoon freshly grated nutmeg

Dash of ground cloves

1 large Granny Smith apple, peeled, cored, and thinly sliced

2 large Cortland apples, peeled, cored, and thinly sliced

2 large McIntosh apples, peeled, cored, and thinly sliced

2 tablespoons cold unsalted butter, diced

$^1/_2$ lemon

EGG WASH AND FINISHING

1 large egg

1 tablespoon heavy cream

1 tablespoon sugar

1. Preheat the oven to 450°F. Line the bottom of a 9-inch glass pie plate with one of the pie crust sheets.
2. In a large bowl, sift together the sugar, flour, salt, nutmeg, and cloves. Whisk together until thoroughly combined. Add the apple slices to the bowl and toss until the apples are completely coated.

3. Fill the lined pie plate with the apple slices, arranging them as compactly as possible. Depending on the size of the apples you've used, you may have some left over.

4. Spread the butter pieces evenly over the apples. Squeeze the lemon over the apples, being careful to catch and discard the seeds.

5. Center the second crust on top of the pie. Press the edges of the top and bottom crust together, then use a fork to make a uniform pattern all the way around the edge. Trim any extra crust around the edge of the pie. Slice three slits in the top to allow steam to escape.

6. Wrap the edge of the pie crust with a wide strip of aluminum foil to prevent the edges from burning. Bake for 15 minutes, then reduce the oven temperature to 350°F and bake for 35 minutes more.

7. In a small bowl, whisk together the egg and cream for the egg wash. Remove the pie from the oven and remove the foil. Brush the top of the pie with the egg wash, sprinkle the sugar over the top, and bake for 15 minutes more.

8. Transfer the pie to a wire rack and let cool for at least 10 minutes before serving.

BASICS

Every home cook should have a few tried-and-true standards, such as sauces, that can be used in lots of different ways. These are usually component elements of other recipes, but let your imagination be your guide and we bet you can find brand-new uses for these.

MEAT SAUCE

A hearty meat sauce is a must-have for anyone who wants to do pasta proud. Originally called sugo di carne *in the Old World, and "Sunday gravy" in the New, every Italian family on the block took pride in putting their own spin on basic meat sauce. The sturdy Irish—all the clans on which the Reagans are based—who grew up next to those families knew better than anyone the value of a good meat sauce. The heart of this one is flavorful Italian sausage, but you can put your own signature on it by substituting turkey sausage or ground chicken. If you use the latter, add a sprinkling of crushed red pepper flakes in step 2.* **Makes about 6 cups sauce**

½ pound loose hot Italian sausage (or remove the casing from links)
2 tablespoons extra-virgin olive oil
1 large Vidalia onion, chopped
3 garlic cloves, minced
1 tablespoon chopped fresh flat-leaf parsley
1 teaspoon dried oregano

Pinch of dried savory
Two 28-ounce cans whole peeled San Marzano tomatoes
Kosher salt and freshly ground black pepper

1. In a large saucepan over medium-high heat, brown the sausage, breaking it up as it cooks. Once the sausage has browned, drain the grease.
2. Heat the olive oil in a 6-quart pot. Add the onion and garlic and sauté until soft. Add the sausage, parsley, oregano, and savory and cook for 1 minute.
3. Add the tomatoes and bring to a boil. Reduce the heat to maintain a simmer and break up the tomatoes with a wooden spoon. Simmer for 2 hours.
4. Taste and season with the salt and pepper as needed. Remove from the heat and use immediately, or let cool for at least 15 minutes before refrigerating or freezing.

LEMON MARINADE

*The fresh and bright combination of honey, citrus, and olive oil gives this marinade a Mediterranean twist. That makes it perfect for skinless, lean white-meat chicken cuts like the bone-in chicken breast in the recipe. The marinade's acid helps the meat absorb the light natural flavors, perking up the chicken without adding heavy notes or boosting calories or fat. The wonderful thing about this recipe is that it's so easy and quick to put together—perfect for trouble-free cookout prep. Keep in mind that this marinade is also a great choice for any white-fleshed fish from cod to sole, and you can even use it to add a little zest to your pork medallions. **Makes ³/₄ cup marinade (about enough for 1 pound of poultry)***

MARINADE

½ cup extra-virgin olive oil

1 tablespoon honey

1 lemon, thinly sliced

5 sprigs fresh rosemary

3 garlic cloves, chopped

½ teaspoon kosher salt

2 bone-in chicken breasts

1. Make the marinade: Combine all the ingredients for the marinade in a large bowl and mix together. Transfer to a 1-gallon resealable plastic bag.
2. Add the chicken and seal the bag. Put the bag inside a second resealable bag to protect against leakage, and refrigerate.
3. Marinate the chicken for at least 30 minutes or up to overnight, turning the bag occasionally.
4. Remove the chicken from the refrigerator and let sit at room temperature for 20 to 30 minutes.
5. Preheat the oven to 350°F. Line a baking sheet with aluminum foil and set a wire rack on top. (If you don't have a rack, use 1-inch-thick lemon slices or red potato halves.)
6. Remove the chicken from the bags and let any excess marinade drain off. Discard the remaining marinade. Bake the chicken on the rack for 45 to 60 minutes, or until the internal temperature registers 165°F on an instant-read thermometer.

SWEET GREEN MARINADE

This marinade has the wonderful combination of sweet and tangy that just makes you glad to have taste buds. It's also as simple as can be—all you need is a couple of minutes and a blender (or a food processor if you don't have a blender handy). In a finely balanced mixture of ingredients, the distinctive flavor of the fresh chives stands out. You can add extra if you're a fan, without doing any damage to the marinade. **Makes 2 cups marinade**

MARINADE

1½ cups buttermilk

2 tablespoons honey

1 tablespoon chopped fresh chives

1 scallion, chopped

1 cup fresh basil leaves

Finely grated zest of 1½ limes

Juice of 1 lime

1 teaspoon kosher salt

Freshly ground black pepper

2 tablespoons olive oil

2 boneless, skinless chicken breasts

1. Make the marinade: Combine all the ingredients for the marinade in a blender. Blend on medium until smooth. Transfer to a 1-gallon resealable plastic bag.
2. Add the chicken and seal the bag. Put the bag inside a second resealable bag to protect against leakage and refrigerate.
3. Marinate the chicken for at least 30 minutes and up to overnight, turning the bag occasionally.
4. Remove the chicken from the refrigerator and let sit at room temperature for 15 minutes.
5. Preheat the oven to 350°F. Line a baking sheet with aluminum foil and set a wire rack on top. (If you don't have a rack, use 1-inch-thick lemon slices or red potato halves.)
6. Remove the chicken from the bags and let any excess marinade drain off. Discard the remaining marinade. Bake the chicken on the rack for 45 to 60 minutes, or until the internal temperature registers 165°F on an instant-read thermometer.

MARINARA LIKE MOM USED TO MAKE

Marinara is one of the most versatile Italian sauces because it works as well on proteins such as fish as it does on all kinds of pasta. Any great marinara sauce carefully balances a subtle sweetness against the acidity of the tomatoes, to create a rich, fresh flavor riddled with hints of spices and herbs. The secret to this sensational version lies in the San Marzano tomatoes—a unique type of Italian plum tomato that has no equal when it comes to flavor. You might want to double the recipe because this sauce freezes well with no loss in flavor—it will keep for up to two months in the freezer. **Makes 6 cups sauce**

1/4 cup extra-virgin olive oil
6 garlic cloves, minced
1 yellow onion, finely chopped
3 tablespoons chopped fresh flat-leaf parsley
1/2 cup chopped fresh basil
Kosher salt and freshly ground black pepper
1/4 cup high-quality red table wine
Two 28-ounce cans peeled whole San Marzano tomatoes

1. In a large pot over medium–high heat, heat the olive oil. Add the garlic and onion and cook until the onion is soft and the garlic is just beginning to brown.
2. Add the parsley and basil, season with salt and pepper, and cook, stirring, for 1 minute.
3. Add the wine and cook, stirring, for 1 minute more. Stir in the tomatoes and use a wooden spoon to crush them. Cover and simmer for 1½ hours, or until the sauce has thickened and the tomatoes are falling apart. Use immediately, or refrigerate or freeze for future use.

LEMON VINAIGRETTE

There really is no excuse for store-bought dressing. You can whip up your own memorable version with a minimum of fuss and mess. The tartness of fresh lemon drives the flavors in this recipe, but you should always be open to experimenting with your vinaigrettes. (What are you risking other than a couple of minutes and some inexpensive ingredients?) Try using Meyer lemons, or go in a totally different direction with blood oranges. The formula is simple—balance acidity and sweetness and add in accent flavors, all of which make vinaigrettes perfect for kitchen experimentation—so go wild.

Makes 1/3 cup

Finely grated zest of 1/2 lemon
Juice of 1 lemon
1/2 teaspoon sugar
1 teaspoon Dijon mustard
1/2 teaspoon crushed dried oregano
1/4 cup extra-virgin olive oil
Kosher salt and freshly ground black pepper

1. In a small bowl, combine the lemon zest, lemon juice, sugar, mustard, and oregano. Whisk until incorporated.
2. Add the oil in a slow stream, whisking constantly until the vinaigrette is emulsified. Taste and season with the salt and pepper as needed, and adjust the ingredients as preferred.
3. Refrigerate until ready to use. The vinaigrette dressing will keep for up to 5 days.

ROASTED GARLIC

Roasting the "stinking rose" turns an overwhelming flavor into a subtle, sweet luxury on the tongue. Although it is incredibly delicious eaten warm from the oven and smashed on a hunk of country bread, roasted garlic is also an unrivaled flavoring agent. Use it to add magic to your soups, sandwiches, sauces, and other dishes. Some garlic lovers even use it to make ice cream or other desserts. We wouldn't go that far, but there is nothing stopping you!

> 3 large bulbs garlic
> 2 tablespoons extra-virgin olive oil

1. Preheat the oven to 350°F.
2. Cut the tips off the garlic bulbs, exposing the ends of the cloves. Drizzle the oil all over the garlic and rub it in to ensure each bulb is completely coated.
4. Wrap each bulb in aluminum foil. Roast for 1 hour, or until the exposed cloves are deep amber.
5. Set the bulbs aside until cool enough to handle, then squeeze them from the closed end to push out the roasted cloves. Smash the cloves and spread on French bread, or jar the garlic and refrigerate for later use.

CHICKEN CUTLETS

*This is an ideal way to dress chicken up—especially if the kids have grown a little tired of plain, old chicken breasts. The breading adds crunch and flavor to the mild chicken, and the finished cutlets can be used in many different ways—from cheesy chicken Parmesan to chicken hero sandwiches (pair it with the Marinara like Mom Used to Make on page 248). But a freshly cooked chicken cutlet is just as nice all by itself, served simply with a squeeze of fresh lemon. **Serves 4***

4 boneless, skinless chicken breasts
Kosher salt and freshly ground black pepper
1 cup all-purpose flour
3 large eggs
1½ cups bread crumbs
¼ cup grated Parmesan cheese
¼ teaspoon dried oregano
¼ cup olive oil

1. On a sturdy work surface, sandwich each chicken breast between two sheets of heavy-duty wax paper. Using a kitchen mallet or the bottom of a cast-iron pan, pound the breasts until they are each about ¼ inch thick. Season each cutlet with salt and pepper.
2. Set up a breading station next to the stovetop: Put the flour in one shallow dish. Beat the eggs with a teaspoon of water and put them into a second shallow dish. Thoroughly mix the bread crumbs, Parmesan, and oregano in a third shallow dish.
3. Dredge a cutlet in the flour and shake off any excess. Dunk it in the egg until it is well coated and let the excess drip off. Press it into the bread crumbs all around, so that it is coated on both sides. Shake off any excess and transfer the cutlet to a clean plate. Repeat with the remaining cutlets.

4. In a large saucepan over medium-high heat, heat the olive oil. Cook the cutlets until golden brown and cooked through, about 4 minutes per side. Work in batches to avoid overcrowding the pan, and add more olive oil as necessary.

5. Remove the cutlets to a plate lined with paper towels and let them cool for at least 5 minutes before serving.

SANDWICH OPTIONS

A chicken Parmesan sandwich is just one more classic offering courtesy of the corner pizza places in Brooklyn. To make your genuine version, place a Chicken Cutlet (page 251) on a baking sheet and top it with a slice of prosciutto. Put a layer of sliced mozzarella on top of the prosciutto, and top with a dollop of Marinara like Mom Used to Make (page 248). Heat in a preheated 425°F oven until the cheese melts and starts to brown. Meanwhile, spread a light coating of sauce on both cut faces of a hoagie roll. Slide the chicken onto the roll and enjoy!

MARINADE FOR GRILLED STEAK

There are two reasons to use a marinade when grilling your next steak: flavoring and tenderizing. This one does both in high style. The balanced blend of savory and sweet adds subtle flavor while still letting the hearty taste of the steak shine through. More important, a long soak in this concoction will break down the fibers that make a tough steak tender. **Makes about 1 cup (enough for 2 large steaks)**

1/3 cup red wine vinegar
1/3 cup canola oil
2 tablespoons honey
1 tablespoon Worcestershire sauce
1 teaspoon ground mustard
1 teaspoon dried oregano
1/2 teaspoon freshly ground black pepper
3 scallions, finely chopped
2 garlic cloves, minced
Steak of your choice

In a large bowl, combine all the ingredients except for the steak. Whisk until thoroughly incorporated. Pour the marinade over the steak in a small glass container. Cover and refrigerate for 8 to 24 hours, turning occasionally. Naturally tender cuts needs less marinating time. For example, a sirloin steak would need only 2 hours. Grill as desired.

GRILLED CHICKEN BREASTS

Although they are perhaps the simplest thing to come off a grill, grilled chicken breasts are incredibly versatile. They are low-fat, healthy options all by themselves, but they can also be chopped up and mixed into your favorite chicken salad recipe. Chop or slice the breasts to add a bit of protein to an otherwise vegetable-rich salad. Or cover with slices of low-fat mozzarella and marinara and tuck under the broiler until the cheese melts, for a healthy version of chicken Parmesan (see box page 252). **Serves 4**

Four 6-ounce boneless, skinless chicken breast halves
Kosher salt and freshly ground black pepper
1 tablespoon fresh lemon juice
¼ cup extra-virgin olive oil

1. Rinse the chicken and pat it dry. Wrap two bricks in aluminum foil, shiny-side out.
2. Season the chicken with salt and pepper. In a large bowl, combine the lemon juice and oil and whisk until emulsified. Add the chicken to the bowl and flip the breasts until entirely coated. Refrigerate, covered, for 1 hour.
3. Preheat a grill or grill pan over medium-high heat. Make sure the grill or pan is clean, and use a ball of wadded paper towel soaked in canola oil to oil the grates or pan.
4. When the grates or grill pan are hot, add the breasts, in pairs, next to each other. Set a brick over each pair. Grill for 3 to 4 minutes until well seared, then flip the breasts and replace the bricks. Grill for 5 minutes more and check with an instant-read thermometer. The chicken temperature should register 160°F.
5. Let the breasts rest for 5 minutes before slicing or cutting. Or allow to cool to room temperature before covering and refrigerating for later use.

BLUE BLOODS FAMILY DINNER MENU

We've filled this book with a wealth of recipes that should make any meal special, but they shine extra bright on the special-occasion dinner table. Putting together a special occasion can be a bit overwhelming, so we decided to jot down some of our favorite party and holiday menus for you. You can also use these as launch pads for your own creativity, mixing and matching as you see fit.

NEW YEAR'S FUN

Ushering out an old year and bringing in a new one calls for food that is light and lively. You want to set a table that goes well with a bottle or four of bubbly, and keeps the mood upbeat, celebratory, and fun. That's why this menu includes simple, rich flavors that eat easily, can be served as a buffet, and don't slow you down for all the dancing you'll want to be doing.

Shrimp Cocktail (page 75)
Salad Caprese (page 59)
Pasta Primavera (page 149)
Sautéed Leeks (page 175)
Roulade Léontine (page 228)

A ROMANTIC VALENTINE'S DINNER

When love is in the air, you need a meal to linger over. Simple, strong flavors and dishes that are easy to prepare and won't take a lot to time (or cleanup) are key. We selected dishes for a variety of flavors and textures, to keep things interesting. A bottle of red wine and a dozen roses are all you need to make this meal complete.

Caesar Salad (page 57)
Bruschetta with Tomatoes and Basil (page 69)
Grilled T–Bone Steak (page 135)
Sweet Brussels Sprouts (page 201)
Nikki's Red Velvet Cupcakes (page 225)

ST. PADDY'S DAY HOORAH

You don't have to be a Reagan to know how fun St. Patrick's Day can be. It's the one day of the year on which everybody is Irish. It's also a great excuse for a fun shindig with dyed beer and hearty food that keeps the spirit of the Emerald Isle alive. *Erin go Bragh!*

Super-Simple Macaroni Salad (page 36)
Corned Beef and Cabbage with Guinness (page 99)
Irish Soda Bread (page 197)
Shortbread and Irish Coffee (page 231)

EASTER

Yes, it's supposed to be about church, but we all know Easter means egg hunts and a big family dinner as well. As two mothers, we're big fans of tradition, so we've stuck with the traditional Easter ham, and a mix of hearty flavors and textures as supporting flavors. These dishes all split the difference between the earthy, filling flavors of winter, and the lighter nature of springtime dishes.

Potato-Leek Soup (page 19)
Glazed Ham (page 119)
Creamed Spinach (page 179)
Roasted Potatoes (page 173)
Strawberry Shortcakes (page 211)

MOTHER'S DAY

Mom deserves the best you can give her, and we should know because we're both moms. The nicest present for any mother is something handmade. The kids can paint a picture or make a piece of bead jewelry, but the rest of the crew should spell mom in the kitchen and make something decadent that she wouldn't make for herself.

Classic Waldorf Salad (page 41)
Green Beans Amandine (page 205)
Veal Scallopini (page 134)
Mashed Potatoes (page 199)
Pecan Pie (page 209)

MEMORIAL DAY

Kicking off the summer season with an observance to respect the military heroes of our country is also the chance to kick off the grilling season with some tried-and-true summer flavors. This menu showcases dishes that can be prepared ahead of time, and others that don't take much time or effort in any case. All the more time you can spend enjoying the sunshine!

Barbecue-Perfect Coleslaw (page 58)
Pigs in a Blanket (page 65)
Grilled Chicken Breasts (page 254)
London Broil (page 117)
Cheesecake with NYPD Blue Topping (page 215)

FOURTH-OF-JULY PICNIC

Picnics, pick-up baseball games, and parades. Meals on the Fourth of July are all about easy, no-fuss dining. That said, the grill has to be working overtime if you're really going to call it a successful Independence Day celebration. So we've included two grilled favorites—burgers and flank steak.

Picnic Potato Salad (page 37)
Super-Simple Macaroni Salad (page 36)
Deviled Pickled Eggs (page 191)
Flank Steak (page 169)
The Ultimate, Over-the-Top, Ode-to-Danny-Reagan Bacon
    Cheeseburger (page 145)
Carrot Cake (page 223)

LABOR DAY

Bringing summer to a close can be a little melancholy, but you make it a lot less so when you gather fresh, end-of-summer produce in some fantastically flavorful dishes. These are also simple dishes to put together because we'd rather see you enjoying the last summer holiday than spend it slaving away in the kitchen.

Fresh Corn-and-Pepper Salad (page 29)
Grilled Chicken Breasts (page 254)
Cornbread (page 184)
Berry Cobbler (page 221)

THE MEMORABLE THANKSGIVING

Thanksgiving is all about family, relaxing, eating, and combining all three into heartwarming memories. Food is the star of the holiday. So gather the tribe, invite solo friends, fire up the stove, and get to work on a feast that no one will soon forget.

Spinach, Avocado, and Orange Salad (page 51)
The Thanksgiving Turkey (page 157)
Buttermilk Biscuits (page 187)
Cranberry Sauce (page 198)
Persimmons with Pomegranate (page 177)
Candied Yams (page 178)
Roasted Garlic Stuffing (page 174)
Pumpkin Pie Two Ways (page 217)

A VERY MERRY (AND TASTY) CHRISTMAS

Christmas can be such a busy time of the year, and there's so much pomp and circumstance around that particular holiday that it's easy to lose sight of what the holiday should really be about (well, besides celebrating a certain birth)—spending time with people you love. And what better way to spend that time, than a long leisurely dinner full of chatting and laughing?

Caesar Salad (page 57)
Stuffed Tomatoes (page 183)
Standing Rib Roast with Cipollini Onion Sauce (page 105)
Popovers (page 189)
Roasted Root Vegetables (page 195)
Minty Peas (page 202)
Roulade Léontine (page 228)

HAPPY BIRTHDAY CELEBRATION

Another year has flown by and it's time to put another candle on the Drugstore Cake. No matter whose birthday it is, make sure the meal says congratulations! This is the perfect time to splurge on dishes that are just a little—or maybe a lot—decadent.

Baked Goat Cheese Salad (page 34)
Shrimp Cocktail (page 75)

Roasted Pork Loin (page 107)
Green Beans Amandine (page 205)
Drugstore Cake (page 233)

THE FUN WEEKNIGHT SURPRISE

Every once in a while you just have to make a celebration out of a Wednesday, or put some excitement into that plain old Tuesday night. Shut off the phone and TV, power down the computers and iPads, and gather around the table for an unexpectedly fun dinner.

Simple Three-Lettuce Dinner Salad (page 27)
Pitch-Perfect Pizza (page 111)
Carrot Cake (page 223)

QUICK AND HEALTHY

It seems like you never have the luxury of extra time, but that doesn't mean you should default to fast food. You can fit a healthy meal into your lifestyle, no matter how frantic that lifestyle makes you. Whip up this vitamin- and fiber-packed meal, and recharge your batteries for whatever comes next on your schedule.

Vegetarian Couscous Salad (page 47)
Green Beans Amandine (page 205)
Grilled Chicken Breasts (page 254)

INDEX

V

Veal

  Osso Buco, 126–127

  Veal Scallopini, 134

Vegetarian Couscous Salad, 47–48

Vinaigrette, Lemon, 249

W

Wahlberg, Donnie, 22, 74, 219

Y

Yams, Candied, 178

Yankee Bean Soup, 21–22

Z

Ziti, Baked, 93–94